What would the world be like without art? Here's to all of you who share your artistic talents with us. You make our world more colorful. More meaningful. More satisfying.

Deloitte & Touche proudly salutes the Denver Confluence of the Arts.

Deloitte & Touche LLP

We Listen. We Deliver.

1560 Broadway
Suite 1800
Denver, CO 80202
(303) 837-3000

Deloitte Touche Tohmatsu International

Founders

Brownstein Hyatt Farber & Strickland, P.C.

Byerly & Company, Inc.

Columbia/HCA Healthcare Corporation
    Aurora Regional Medical Center
    North Suburban Medical Center
    Rose Medical Center

Denver Metro Convention & Visitors Bureau

Elitch Gardens

HealthONE

Hensel Phelps Construction Co.

Key Bank of Colorado

Robert Koropp

Loews Giorgio Hotel

The Oxford Hotel

Pepsi-Cola Company

ProServe Corporation

RE/MAX Mountain States

Rose Health Care System—
    A part of the Columbia/HCA
    Healthcare Corporation

University of Denver

Founders

Brownstein Hyatt Farber & Strickland, P.C.

Byerly & Company, Inc.

Columbia/HCA Healthcare Corporation
Aurora Regional Medical Center
North Suburban Medical Center
Rose Medical Center

Denver Metro Convention & Visitors Bureau

Elitch Gardens

HealthONE

Hensel Phelps Construction Co.

Key Bank of Colorado

Robert Koropp

Loews Giorgio Hotel

The Oxford Hotel

Pepsi-Cola Company

ProServe Corporation

RE/MAX Mountain States

Rose Health Care System—
A part of the Columbia/HCA
Healthcare Corporation

University of Denver

Denver
Confluence
of the ARTS

Benefactors

A.B. Hirschfeld Press, Inc.

9NEWS/9KUSA

Patrons

Deloitte & Touche LLP

Embassy Suites Hotel & Athletic Club
at Denver Place

Great-West Life & Annuity Insurance Company

Johnson & Higgins of Colorado

Samsonite Corporation

US West

Friends

KVOD-FM Radio

Marcus & Millichap Real Estate Investment
Brokerage Company of Denver

Museum of Outdoor Arts

Piper Jaffray Inc.

Price Waterhouse LLP

The Publishing House

Robinson Dairy Inc.

St. Mary Land & Exploration Company

Shames-Makovsky Realty Company

Wong Strauch Architects

Swanson Rink

Denver
Confluence
of the ARTS

WRITTEN BY

JEFF BRADLEY

JANE FUDGE

JENNIFER HEATH

MARILYNNE S. MASON

PUBLISHED BY

MERIDIAN

INTERNATIONAL, INC.

Published by
Meridian International, Inc.
4155 E. Jewel Avenue, #707
Denver, CO 80222
303-692-1901

For Meridian International, Inc.—
Mike Hillis, *President and CEO*
Steve Furner, *Vice President of Production*
Ellis Child, *Vice President of Finance*
Bart Barica, *Vice President
  of Corporate Publications*
Scott Garrett, *Vice President of Sales*
Bonnie Kopinski, *Vice President of
  Human Resources*

Cover photograph, "Soundscape,"
by Robert Koropp, Golden, Colorado.

ISBN: 0-9635893-0-X

Printed in the U.S.A.

We are indebted to the Denver Mayor's Office of Art, Culture and Film for its invaluable
contribution—verifying facts, proofing and suggesting resources. Special recognition and
applause go to Lezlie Sokolik, designer, and Elizabeth Emmett, editor, for their tireless
attention to the infinite number of details that it took to complete this book. Another
round of applause goes to Vicki Andersen, copy chief, for doing what needed doing.

Thank you.

Margaret Shields Marti
Director of Publishing

photo © James Baca

The Soul of the City

If people make up the heart of a vibrant community, then its soul is revealed through its commitment to arts, culture and diversity.

In Denver that commitment is embodied in Mayor Wellington E. Webb's Commission on Art, Culture and Film (MCACF), a citizens group of art, cultural, business and community leaders, and in the staff members at the Mayor's Office of Art, Culture and Film (MOACF). Together these supporters of the arts coordinate and enhance artistic and cultural activities, and serve as catalysts for events and programs that encourage diversity throughout the community.

Under the vision of the Mayor and the Commission, the MOACF works to foster public art, special events, program initiatives, film and television production, education, funding and marketing.

Each year, MOACF offers technical assistance and/or support to more than 50 special events and produces the annual Colorado Performing Arts Festival. This weekend event attracts more than 60,000 people and features nearly 100 performances, workshops, demonstrations and hands-on activities showcasing the state's finest performing artists. Film and television production companies work with MOACF staff on site selection, permitting and other needs, while educational institutions and community groups look to the MOACF to support educational programs that focus on arts and culture.

MOACF coordinates the publication and distribution of *Arts Montage*, a quarterly publication devoted to the arts activities in the African-American, Asian Pacific, Latino, Hispanic and Native American communities. Both the MCACF and MOACF, with the enthusiastic support of the community, work to preserve and enrich the vibrant cultural tapestry that continues to play a major role in the life of people of Denver.

Denver City Council

Wellington E. Webb
Mayor
Deborah L. "Debbie" Ortega
President 1994-1996
Allegra "Happy" Haynes
President Pro Tem
Dennis Gallagher
T.J. "Ted" Hackworth
Ramona Martinez
Joyce Foster
Polly Flobeck
Sue Casey
Bill Himmelman
Hiawatha Davis Jr.
Edward P. Thomas
Cathy Reynolds
Susan Barnes-Gelt

The Denver Mayor's Commission on Art, Culture and Film

Joe Franzgrote, *Chairman*
Jose Aguayo
Karen Beard
Mel Carter
Noël R. Congdon
Jill Irvine Crow
Pamela Endsley
Taffy Lee
Henry E. Lowenstein
Laura Loyacono
Michael Roybal
Ron Schwab
Lucille "Dutchess" Scheitler
First Lady Wilma J. Webb
Max Wiley
Susan Wick
Stella Yu

The Denver Mayor's Office of Art, Culture and Film

Joyce Oberfeld
Director
Rosemary Rodriguez
Deputy Director
Ron Pinkard
Deputy Director
Elizabeth Brownsberger
Public Art Consultant-
Denver International Airport
Gloria Campbell
Special Events Coordinator
Greg Esser
Public Art Administrator
Brenda LaCota
Staff Assistant
d'Alene Meardon
Assistant Special Events Coordinator
Bruce Thomson
Art Program Administrator-
Denver International Airport

Jennifer Heath

Jennifer Heath, a longtime advocate of Colorado arts, has written with authority about the field for books and periodicals. Her work is described as "meaningful, passionate and sometimes witty," by Tom Wolfe at the *Rocky Mountain News*. Heath is the author of *Black Velvet: The Art We Love to Hate* and curated a national touring show of the same name. She also has written three children's books and the forthcoming illustrated novel *El Repelente or The Anti-Nuke Antics of Anabela*.

Jane Fudge

Jane Fudge is a Denver-based visual arts and film critic who has written for *The Muse (Colorado Arts)*, *Westword*, the *Denver Post*, the *Boulder Camera* and many other local and regional publications. She is a graduate of the University of Colorado at Denver and is on the staff of the Modern and Contemporary Art Department of the Denver Art Museum, where she has curatorial responsibility for more than 1,200 19th-century American landscape photographs.

Jeff Bradley

Jeff Bradley is critic-at-large for the *Denver Post*, covering the Colorado Symphony, Opera Colorado and music events around the Rockies, as well as jazz and folk music, news and features about the arts. A trained musician, he lectures at the University of Denver Humanities Institute and elsewhere. Before coming to Denver in 1989, he spent 20 years as an Associated Press correspondent in Europe, Asia and Canada.

Marilynne S. Mason

Marilynne S. Mason, a graduate of UCLA Theatre Arts Department, holds a master's degree in filmmaking from UCLA film school. She is currently the theater critic for Denver's third largest paper, the weekly *Westword*. She wrote for the *Christian Science Monitor* for six years as contributing arts writer, film and theater critic and reporter. She has written film essays for the *World Monitor Magazine* and *ArtSpace*, and art criticism for the *Rocky Mountain News* and *Colorado Expressions* magazine. Her work has appeared in *American Theatre Magazine*, the *Denver Post*, *Variety*, the *Washington Post*, the *Los Angeles Times* and the *Hollywood Reporter*.

Robert Koropp

Photographer Robert Koropp's photo "Soundscape" graces the cover of *Denver, Confluence of the Arts*; several of his photos also appear inside the book. Acclaimed for both advertising and fine arts photography, Koropp has had more than 50 one-man shows in the United States and abroad, and a larger number of joint shows. He also has taught and lectured extensively.

He currently is involved in what he calls "conceptual imagery"—things he can feel or imagine but that he can't see with the physical eye until he has devised a way to put them down on film. He calls them "visions of the mind's eye."

It might be said that in Denver artistic expression began millions of years ago when the earth created the breathtaking landscape of the Rocky Mountains. Behind the confluence of the Platte River and Cherry Creek, where Denver was founded, the mountains are brushed with a palette of constantly changing color, light and shadow.

From the time of the earliest Native American occupants, our region has been a **crossroads** of cultures and ideas. When the first non-native settlers arrived from Mexico and Spain, native cultures were thriving. Ute, Arapaho, Cheyenne, Kiowa and others had developed unique artistic traditions and techniques. Within a few decades, America's great westward migration drew newcomers from around the world to the Queen City of the Plains. Among the new arrivals were artists and craftspeople who taught and learned new skills, techniques, music, dances and performing traditions.

There were clashes of culture, too; some violent. But with time's passage, the cultures converged to form today's vibrant and thriving metropolitan Denver. **Together** we have come to value the artistic and spiritual heritage of all cultures. We are a community of diverse traditions with a shared future that is further enriched as more people flow into the confluence.

Denver's **appreciation** for the arts is immediately apparent in its architecture and urban design. Our Civic Center, modeled on the classical Greek style of architecture, is the cornerstone of a system of broad boulevards and scenic parkways. The historic is complemented by the modern; the Denver Art Museum is home to one of the foremost collections of native arts found in any museum. Next door, our new $72 million Central Library features the largest public library collection of Western Americana.

Nearby is the Denver Performing Arts Complex, America's largest collection of theaters under one roof. In the foothills, Denver's Red Rocks Amphitheatre, formed by sandstone pinnacles rising dramatically skyward, is a stunning geological masterpiece, and also happens to be a wonderful place to hear a concert.

Denver is a city of world-class symphonic music, ballet, opera, community theater, performing arts and visual arts. We are home to scores of cultural institutions, such as the Black American West Museum and the Museo de las Americas. Annual cultural events include the Denver International Film Festival and the Cherry Creek Arts Festival. Dozens of other citywide and neighborhood ethnic and cultural fairs and festivals attract thousands of participants.

The arts and culture are **so important to us** in Denver that we voted to allocate one tenth of one percent of metro-area sales tax for our scientific and cultural organizations. Approved during a time of general tax resistance, the measure generates $20 million annually for the arts and cultural institutions.

We've also established a citywide ordinance requiring that all city construction projects having budgets that exceed $1 million allocate one percent of the estimated budget for public art. Because of this **commitment**, the magnificent new Denver International Airport boasts the largest single-facility public art program in the United States.

We Denverites are **proud** of our city. The culture and character of our community has its roots in those people who crossed the plains hundreds of years ago. Today at the crossroads of our nation you will find Denver, Colorado, a rapidly flowing confluence of commerce, culture and creativity.

To those who made this book possible, the private citizens and public-minded companies that contributed their time, and to those whose **creativity** made this book come to life, we express our gratitude and our admiration.

And to First Lady Wilma J. Webb, whose efforts as a chairperson of the Mayor's Commission on Art, Culture and Film established a clear sense of focus and new spirit of inclusion for the arts in Denver, I extend my deepest personal and professional appreciation.

Wellington E. Webb,
Mayor of Denver

Building a City
by Jane Fudge

The first crude board structures of the mining hamlet that would be named "Denver City" were built at the junction of the South Platte River and Cherry Creek in the late 1850s. Since then, Denver has more than once flooded out, burned down and bulldozed itself flat. For this still-young metropolis, architecture has a special meaning. Denver's buildings, new and old, are potent symbols of the city's longing for permanence and substance, and affirmations of civic pride and culture.

LARIMER SQUARE
PHOTO COURTESY OF
THE DENVER METRO
CONVENTION &
VISITORS BUREAU

DENVER'S COLORADO
CONVENTION CENTER
PHOTO COURTESY OF
THE DENVER METRO
CONVENTION &
VISITORS BUREAU

15

The boom-and-bust cycles that dominate the economies of the West have affected Denver's architectural development as well as every other aspect of the city's life. In times of prosperity, Denver has built lavishly, awarding commissions to local and imported architectural talent alike, creating neighborhoods, schools and parks, and investing in public works. When its fortunes have been at low ebb, the city waits, catching its breath, enjoying the most recent harvest while dreaming of the next.

Coors Field, home of the Colorado Rockies, forms the cornerstone of the revitalized LoDo.

PHOTO BY NATE COX

Surprisingly, the self-styled "Queen City of the Plains" remains a virtual compendium of American architecture, with entire neighborhoods and many important buildings left intact, each speaking in a vocabulary of style as distinctive as the many languages and accents of its people.

Bands of succeeding architectural forms and fashions, like the growth rings of a tree, are circumscribed by Denver's rippling metropolitan borders. Rows of austere "stick" houses give way to grander buildings of stone and brick in the Romanesque revival of Henry Richardson, and those to houses and churches inspired by the theories of Louis Sullivan.

Blocks of bungalows follow blocks of more ostentatious beaux arts residences, and staid neoclassical edifices are passed in their turn by sleek buildings in the moderne or art deco idiom. On the small campus of the University of Denver, nearly every generation has added at least one building to the prevailing style of the times; today it is a mini-history of American architecture in brick and stone.

Denver's Lower Downtown (LoDo, for short), once the city's dusty, noisy commercial heart, has matured into a district distinguished by the reserved expressions of Romanesque revival and prairie school architecture, solidly mercantile, honest, fundamentally optimistic. These buildings—among metropolitan Denver's oldest—now enjoy a second or third springtime as live-in lofts, art galleries, furniture showrooms and restaurants. Larimer Square, one of the most successful "old town" renovations in the nation, started here in the 1960s. Its streets remain as crowded with office workers, tourists, history buffs and students as they once were with gold-seekers, cattle queens and mining barons in Denver's wildest pioneer days.

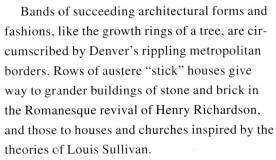

Presiding over LoDo is Coors Field, the huge new major league baseball stadium. The stadium's design and materials, its red brick facings and old-fashioned green-painted seats, allow this giant to fit itself comfortably into the squares of low-rise buildings that cluster along the oldest streets in Denver.

Across Cherry Creek from LoDo is the Auraria Higher Education Center (AHEC). It comprises the urban campuses of the University of Colorado, Metropolitan State College and the Community College of Denver, and takes its name from Auraria, Denver City's gold-rush era rival. At one time Auraria's growth and prosperity promised to outstrip Denver's, but in 1860 the two towns merged and Auraria became a west Denver neighborhood dominated by successive waves of newcomers: Germans, Irish, Jews and Hispanics.

By the 1960s Auraria had fallen on hard times and was in danger of being erased altogether by demolition projects. Saved from extinction, AHEC's clusters of severely practical academic buildings are relieved by greenways and footpaths and many landmarks of old Auraria, such as the stately middle-class residences of Ninth Street Park, and mission-style Saint Cajetan's and Gothic revival Saint Elizabeth's churches. The old Shearith Israel Synagogue, where Denver's Jewish community worshipped in the 19th century, houses an art gallery. The vast Tivoli Brewery, once Auraria's biggest industry, has been restored as AHEC's student center.

LoDo and the AHEC anchor the improvements to the once-neglected Platte Valley. Coors Field's 1995 opening season brought thousands of Rockies fans to town, while Elitch's, Denver's pioneer amusement park, now sits next to AHEC after a century in the city's northwest quadrant. Elitch's fantasy of antique carousels and state-of-the-art roller coasters provides a colorful contrast—and a certain amount of temptation—to studious campus life.

Denver's recurring petroleum booms and the burgeoning of post-World War II suburban

THE BIG NEW CENTRAL LIBRARY

Jane Fudge

In 1990 Denver again made a substantial and farsighted investment in its future by approving—by a landslide—a $91.6 million bond issue to pay for improvements to the heavily used Denver Public Library system. The funds provided for four new branch libraries and the renovation of 15 historic branches scattered around the city, but the most dramatic result is the new Central Library, which opened in 1995.

The seven-story building, by internationally renowned architect Michael Graves and the Denver firm of Klipp Colussy Jenks DuBois, integrates the old Burnham Hoyt Library and trebles its size to 540,000 square feet. DPL Central echoes the shapes and tonalities of Denver's downtown skyline with staggered rooflines and colorful exterior facings of sandstone and limestone; Denver snows will eventually weather copper-clad pavilions and decorative elements into muted greens and browns. Inside the four-story central hall, acclaimed artist Ed Ruscha's 70-panel series of paintings combining words and images about the West overlooks the reference center and checkout desk. The series was commissioned by the City and County of Denver.

Truly a multi-use building, the Central Library has not only 47 miles of shelves to browse but also a gift shop, conference center and art gallery. Despite its imposing size, the library's interior spaces are informal and friendly, sporting vividly patterned carpets, polished wooden doors and balustrades, and lots of windows through which to enjoy city and mountain views—just in case one hasn't found something to read.

The sweeping vistas of Schlessman Hall (upper left), the sturdy architecture of the Gates Western History Room (left) and Edward Ruscha's epic artwork make a showplace of the Central Library of the Denver Public Library.

communities once threatened the viability of the downtown commercial center. Overly zealous renewal projects in the 1960s and 1970s swept away many landmark buildings, frequently replacing them only with parking lots. Gleaming international-style skyscrapers sprouted along Broadway and up and down 17th Street, dwarfing the low-rise financial and hotel districts.

THE ONE-TENTH PERCENT SOLUTION

Jane Fudge

In a visionary vote in 1988, Denver metro area residents overwhelmingly favored the creation of the Scientific and Cultural Facilities District (SCFD). The one-tenth of one percent sales tax, renewed for another decade in 1994, provides a stable source of funding, to the tune of $20 million annually, for some 200 large and small cultural entities that enliven the Front Range.

SCFD money supports activities such as free admission days for families and seniors, and enhanced educational programs and outreach to underserved groups throughout the state by Denver's largest cultural institutions. With support from SCFD funds, more than 2.75 million people each year enjoy free or reduced admissions. In 1992 metro area cultural groups provided more than 1,000 programs targeted to the elderly, minorities, people with disabilities and children—up from 210 in 1989. The Denver Museum of Natural History, Denver Art Museum, Botanic Gardens and Zoological Gardens are all able to reach more Coloradans through SCFD funds. And while the accomplishments of these large institutions are impressive and vital to the public life of the region, more modest arts institutions also make great strides with their share of the one-tenth percent.

With SCFD support, Arvada Center for the Arts and Humanities presented the evocative photographs of octogenarian artist Ruth Bernhard, whose lecture garnered standing-room-only attendance. In Jefferson County the Friends of Dinosaur Ridge used SCFD money to excavate fossil dinosaur tracts, beating out *Jurassic Park* for realism. SCFD's boost to such small but seasoned groups as Colorado Dance Festival, Chicano Humanities and Arts Council, Alternative Arts Alliance, Changing Scene Theatre and the Thornton Arts, Sciences and Humanities Council is not just practical but spiritual, allowing their artists and administrators to dream a little beyond balancing the books. Foothills Art Center in Golden put its SCFD portion to a supremely utilitarian end: The Center got a new roof to keep the weather off the exhibitions.

Startled into action, private citizens, politicians and activist groups, such as Historic Denver, mobilized to ameliorate these trends. Preservation efforts created Larimer Square and protected many other structures. The 16th Street Mall, designed by I.M. Pei and Partners, was developed to restore the tattered city center. The Mall, lined with honey locust and red oak trees, opened in 1982 and spans the length of downtown Denver. It is both pedestrian promenade and transitway, with fountains and benches for passersby and curbed runways for the free motor shuttles that ferry commuters to the bus terminals and lunch-hour shoppers on their errands.

Other downtown stars are the Denver Performing Arts Complex, whose soaring glass canopies shelter several theaters and concert halls, and the Colorado Convention Center, a vast exhibition space with distinctive tiered entrances.

The lively and eclectic tastes of Denver's builders have resulted in a wealth of unique public and private buildings that share the city's streets with distinguished predecessors. Philip Johnson's round-topped Norwest Bank (referred to with skeptical affection as the "cash register building") looms over Mile High Center, built in the 1950s by I.M. Pei, and the Brown Palace Hotel, built by Frank Edbrooke in 1892. Holy Ghost Catholic Church nestles in the angular embrace of Curt Fentress's 1999 Broadway, a skyscraper outlined at night with green fluorescent tubing visible for miles. Across Denver's Civic Center Park, the castellated top of the Denver Art Museum, built by Italian architect Gio Ponti and Denver's James Sudler and Associates in 1971, glistens with a million faceted tiles above the trees of Civic Center Park. Next door is the new Central Library of the Denver Public Library, a postmodern design by Michael Graves and Brian Klipp that features towers and porticoes clad in colored stone, and rotundas that command panoramic views of the Rocky Mountains.

Distant but clearly visible from many of Denver's high-rise buildings, the translucent fiberglass peaks of Denver International Airport's expressionistic roofline, by architects Fentress and Bradburn, evoke the forms of mountains or of Indian lodges shining in the Colorado sun.

In the 1990s Denverites take as much pride in the reuse of old buildings as in new additions to the Denver skyline. Recent successes such as the renovation of Edbrooke's old Denver Dry Goods

building into retail and living spaces, and the renaissance of the sturdy warehouses of Lower Downtown hold the promise of a rich architectural legacy for the next century.

Perhaps the greatest triumph of Denver's architecture and city planning are its public spaces. A system of large and small parks throughout Denver and surrounding counties, many connected by hike-and-bike paths, makes outdoor recreation a simple matter. Thanks largely to Mayor Wellington E. Webb's commitment to preserving dedicated open space in the Central Platte Valley, Commons Park, Rockmont and Gates Park are in varied stages of development. The most pressing challenge to the future of Denver's urban scheme is the successful linking of its multiplex residential, cultural, commercial and recreational facilities while containing pollution and overdevelopment.

Old stalwarts such as City Park, Washington Park and Congress Park have been joined by a new generation of green areas, several of which lie along streams or canals. Tiny, exquisite Creek-

front Park, completed in 1993, is an oasis of quiet beside one of Denver's busiest intersections, Larimer Street and Speer Boulevard. On warm afternoons, winter or summer, skaters and kayakers skim effortlessly along the South Platte River as it hastens to meet Cherry Creek at Confluence Park, past the river walk and amphitheater that mark the spot where Denver's story began.

THE WORLD TRADE CENTER © ROBERT KOROPP, GOLDEN, CO

DENVER INTERNATIONAL AIRPORT
COURTESY OF THE DENVER METRO
CONVENTION & VISITORS BUREAU

Early shot of the Mining Exchange Building
Courtesy of Denver Public Library Western History Department

The Brown Palace Hotel

The Denver Skyline

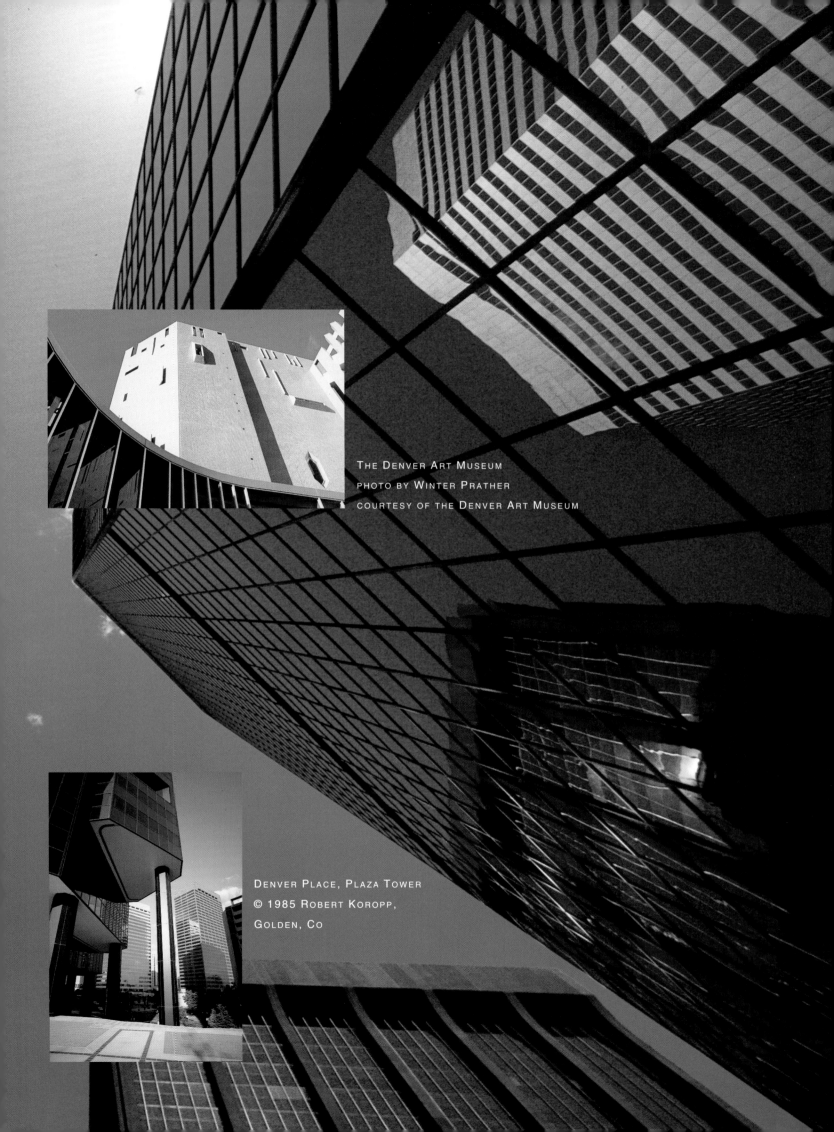

THE DENVER ART MUSEUM
PHOTO BY WINTER PRATHER
COURTESY OF THE DENVER ART MUSEUM

DENVER PLACE, PLAZA TOWER
© 1985 ROBERT KOROPP,
GOLDEN, CO

THE ARCHDIOCESE OF DENVER

PHOTOS © JAMES BACA

musical arts

Magna Opus
by Jeff Bradley

It's been a musical town from the beginning. Home to performers from Paul Whiteman to Judy Collins, Denver has a rich musical heritage stretching back to the 19th century when fortunes were made from Rocky Mountain gold and silver. Whether in opera houses built during those rough-and-ready days, the spectacular open-air surroundings of Red Rocks Amphitheatre or at El Chapultepec bar, where the bebop comes with burritos, there's a diverse year-round menu of classical, pop, jazz and folk music.

"SOUNDSCAPE" © 1995 ROBERT KOROPP
GOLDEN, CO

Legendary Horace Tabor set an early example when he used the profits from his silver mines near Leadville to open Denver's lavish Tabor Grand Opera House in 1881. The Victorian city also sported a Handel and Haydn Society, Quadrille Band and Choral Union.

Enrico Caruso sang at the Municipal Auditorium in 1920, his fee a colossal $12,000, while

The most remarkable musical story of the past decade has been the resurgence of the Colorado Symphony Orchestra, brought back to life by its own musicians after the debt-laden Denver Symphony folded in the spring of 1989. Adopting a new name and a user-friendly approach, the 78-member CSO quickly expanded its budget from an initial $2 million to nearly $7 million in 1995 and appointed Marin Alsop, the country's most prominent woman conductor, as its first music director.

© LASZLO

COURTESY OF CSO

TOP: The Colorado Youth Pops Orchestra nurtures promising young musicians.
BOTTOM: Marin Alsop is credited by many with breathing new life into the Colorado Symphony Orchestra.

the first all-professional Denver Symphony was in place as early as 1934. Local legend tells of the props catching fire during a symphony performance of Wagner's *Die Walkure* at Red Rocks in 1957.

Musical variety today stretches from touring rock superstars to the resident Gamelan Tunas Mekar Balinese Orchestra and the burnished tones of The Denver Brass as well as the world-renowned Takacs String Quartet, artists-in-residence at the University of Colorado in Boulder.

You might see a flamenco show at Littleton's Town Hall Arts Center (a converted fire station), catch a Finnish folk group at the purpose-built Arvada Center for the Arts and Humanities, or hobnob with socialites at the Denver Art Museum's Wednesday night "Top of the Week" fusion jazz party.

The public gets a free sample of the region's artistic depth each September when the city sponsors a Colorado Performing Arts Festival at the Denver Performing Arts Complex, a glass-enclosed maze of theaters near the heart of downtown.

At a time when other orchestras were struggling with huge deficits, the CSO attracted national attention by operating in the black with broad-based community support, including corporate and foundation grants and city sponsorship of free concerts.

At first the CSO was entirely self-governing. The musicians made substantial sacrifices to show they meant business. Their earnings were a paltry $11,000 the first year as they devoted countless hours to business meetings in addition to weekly performances of Beethoven and Brahms.

A board that reflects Denver's cultural diversity was carefully constructed and administrative staff streamlined in a partnership that guarantees musicians a role in every important artistic and business decision. "Wherever I go, people ask me about the Colorado Symphony; they look to us as a national model of how to restructure their own symphony orchestras," conductor Alsop says.

Down-to-earth marketing, $10 "blue jeans" concerts and a lively pops series with performers such as Bobby McFerrin and Mel Torme helped bring a record 225,000 concertgoers to Boettcher Concert Hall in 1994. In addition, a novel series of youth concerts and "Up Close and Musical" visits to the schools reach some 65,000 children a year.

When similar fiscal problems brought the 25-year-old Denver Chamber Orchestra to a halt in 1994, its 30 musicians followed the CSO's example by regrouping as the Chamber Orchestra of the West.

Its Western-flavored acronym—COW—demonstrated an offbeat sense of humor, and a new populist spirit was evident in the ensemble's first concerts. With listeners huddled around candlelit cabaret tables, the orchestra brought Baroque music to the funky Mercury Cafe. Conductor Tom Bloomster introduced a piece by 17th-century French composer Lully by wielding a wooden staff like the one Lully used for conducting. (On one occasion Lully struck his foot by accident, leading to gangrene and one of the most bizarre deaths in music history.) Bloomster wisely resorted to an ordinary baton before giving the downbeat. Another concert found the COW performing Dixieland with the Queen City Jazz Band to a full house at Bethany Lutheran Church.

Launched in 1983 with performances of *La Boheme* starring Placido Domingo and *Otello* featuring James McCracken, Opera Colorado brings international grand opera to Denver each year. Local talents developed by the company include Stephen West and Haojiang Tian, now on the rosters of the New York City Opera and the Metropolitan Opera.

Opera Colorado is the only company in the country presenting its extravaganzas in the round. Its use of circular Boettcher Concert Hall has led to the creation of ingenious modular sets, processions through the aisles and audience-pleasing scenes such as Cherubino literally climbing into the seats to escape from the Countess' bedroom in *The Marriage of Figaro*. Because there was no parapet from which Tosca could make her famous leap, she ended it all with a gun! Stars who have appeared over the years include Pilar Lorengar, Alain Vanzo, Ashley Putnam, James Morris, Sherrill Milnes, Eva Marton, Martina Arroyo, Aprile Millo, Jon Vickers, Justino Diaz and Elizabeth Holleque.

In 1994 company director Nathaniel Merrill and his wife, opera coach Louise Sherman, fulfilled a dream by opening the Joseph & Loretta Law Artist Center, a year-round school for budding opera singers.

REBIRTH OF A SYMPHONY

Jeff Bradley

When the Colorado Symphony Orchestra gave its first concert at McNichols Sports Arena on Oct. 27, 1989, with the help of rock promoter Barry Fey, it was a triumph of will for the musicians of the former Denver Symphony Orchestra, which had folded earlier in the year.

One of those who refused to let the symphony die was principal violist Lee Yeingst, a member of the orchestra since 1960. With other musicians he worked tirelessly to keep the organization alive. Despite announcing his retirement in April 1995, Yeingst remained in the viola section through the 1995-1996 season. He served as both vice-chair of the board of trustees and president of the Colorado Symphony League, which coordinates volunteers.

He looks back on the CSO's unique solution for survival: "Those of us who had been here a number of years were really concerned that a strong artistic resource for the city would just disappear. Like many other orchestras today, the Denver Symphony was a debt-prone organization that just simply could not balance the budget.

Lee Yeingst
COURTESY OF THE COLORADO
SYMPHONY ORCHESTRA
© PILON STUDIO OF PHOTOGRAPHY

"Now we're no longer concerned about just surviving. Our responsibility is to develop one of the nation's leading artistic institutions. We have that potential with the leadership of Marin Alsop and support from the city."

He noted a recent survey in which more than half the people questioned mentioned the Colorado Symphony among Denver's cultural assets.

"We formed a partnership model that includes musicians; staff and volunteers; the board; the Musicians Union; our funders, donors and subscribers; and the man in the street. It's a remarkable achievement and one that's viewed with some wonderment nationally. That's certainly something the city, not just the musicians, can be proud of.

"We've shown that a city can have an arts organization that is first-rate without being a financial burden. That's why I feel pretty good today."

Each summer opera lovers head to the old mining town of Central City, less than an hour west of Denver, where three operas are performed in the 756-seat Central City Opera House, lovingly built in 1878 by Cornish and Welsh miners. The building fell into disrepair in the 1920s but reopened to great acclaim in 1932 with an annual summer festival that has brought

ABOVE: **Chautauqua Auditorium, Boulder**
RIGHT: **Students at the Colorado Youth Instrumental Program**

COURTESY OF THE COLORADO CHAUTAUQUA ASSOC.

COURTESY OF THE COLORADO YOUTH INSTRUMENTAL PROGRAM

Lillian Gish, Mae West and Beverly Sills to Central City. Among today's stars who gained early experience at Central City are baritone Sherrill Milnes and bass Samuel Ramey, who sent in a tape on the odd chance he would be accepted. "I'd never seen an opera until I was taking part in one at Central City," Ramey said.

Restored to its original splendor in the 1980s, the opera house presents everything in English, from *The Student Prince* to *Carmen*. Seasoned professionals perform side-by-side with more than two dozen apprentice and studio artists for whom the summer is a crash course in footlight realities. It's a bit like summer camp for adults. The singers all stay in Victorian homes on the sloping hillsides of the town, where many a

love affair and marriage has ensued.

One of the least-known but most enjoyable musical events in Colorado takes place weekends in the adjacent Teller House, an 1872 Romanesque Revival hotel that doubles as a casino with a steady stream of gamblers trying their luck on the ground-floor slot machines. Here the singers relax after a performance by showing off in front of die-hard operagoers and colleagues. They might belt out a favorite song from *South Pacific* or a difficult aria they wouldn't dare attempt on stage. With good-natured heckling, belly laughs and occasionally some stupendous singing from novices hoping to one day reach the Met, it's an unforgettable experience. Some singers spend the winter as artists-in-residence, touring Colorado's schools.

From opera to avant-garde jazz, the University of Colorado College of Music and University of Denver's Lamont School of Music offer full seasons of public concerts. CU also hosts the annual Boulder Bach Festival, MahlerFest, Lyric Theatre Festival and an Artist Series that brings in such celebrities as Kathleen Battle.

DU hosts an International Guitar Week and Friends of Chamber Music concerts, a volunteer-run series that for 41 years has presented top artists such as the Beaux Arts Trio and Emerson String Quartet.

Denver's network of generous music patrons demonstrated their value most eloquently in 1991 when the Lamont School invited the all-female Moscow String Quartet to spend five years on campus as artists-in-residence. The four women and their families arrived from Russia with little English, little money, no agent and no homes. But volunteers led marathon shopping expeditions and settled the quartet into cozy southeast Denver apartments. After a crash course in English, the women were able to focus on performing, teaching and touring.

Marilyn Horne and Itzhak Perlman are among high-profile artists regularly secured by the semi-professional Boulder Philharmonic, which offers a colorful season of concerts at CU's spacious Macky Auditorium.

Each summer orchestral players from all over the world gather at Chautauqua Park beneath the Flatirons Range on Boulder's western edge for the eight-week Colorado Music Festival. Under founder Giora Bernstein, the 19-year-old festival offers world-class artists and challenging repertoire in the resonant acoustics of Chautauqua Auditorium, a board-and-batten barn built in 1898 as a summer study center.

The festival has a cozy feeling. Musicians and their families stay in summer cottages and take turns hosting post-concert parties. The music-making is first-rate, from Schoenberg rarities to blockbuster pops, and violinist Gil Shaham is among the regular guests. The park itself connects with winding trails that take a visitor up into the diagonal-shaped Flatirons, offering panoramic views of Boulder and metro Denver.

Metro residents also enjoy easy access via I-70 to the summer's prestigious Aspen Music Festival, Bravo! Colorado in Vail, Breckenridge Music Festival and Strings in the Mountains in Steamboat Springs. Many also head south down I-25 to Santa Fe for the region's oldest and most-respected opera festival—and the blue corn tortillas.

Raising their voices together, thousands of dedicated Front Range residents have made Denver a center of excellence for choral singing. It starts early with the Colorado Children's Chorale. Founded in 1974 by conductor Duain Wolfe, the highly professional organization boasts five separate choirs involving a total of 400 kids ages 7 to 13. They have toured nationally and abroad, including two trips to China. A highlight of every Christmas season is the chorale's concert with the Colorado Symphony.

Wolfe, who doubles as choral director for the Chicago Symphony, also trains and conducts the Colorado Symphony Chorus, one of the finest in the country in repertoire ranging from Bach to an annual Gilbert & Sullivan operetta.

Other outstanding choirs include the Opera Colorado Chorus trained by Louise Sherman, the Colorado Choir, Ars Nova Chamber Singers, Denver Gay Men's Chorus, Cherry Creek

Chorale, Colorado Chorale, the Choir of St. John's Cathedral and the Abbey Singers, in addition to exceptionally well-trained gospel and church choirs.

When Eulipions, Denver's African-American theater, put on a gospel version of *Oedipus at Colonus* and the musical *Mahalia's Song* about Mahalia Jackson, audiences were surprised by the quality of local church singers. The wealth of gospel talent is so great, Denver has its own annual Gospel Music Academy awards.

Meanwhile, in the city that produced violin virtuoso Eugene Fodor, the Colorado Young Artists Orchestra and Colorado Youth Symphony offer school-age musicians a chance to perform, while older amateurs have their choice of community orchestras such as the Jefferson Symphony, Arapahoe Philharmonic, Centennial Philharmonic and Littleton Symphony.

As elsewhere in the nation, school music budgets have been cut in Denver, but community efforts are filling the gap. In 1995 the Rocky Mountain Chapter of the American Theater Organ Society installed a computerized organ at East High School where students study the instrument and its many uses.

Since 1993 the Cherry Creek Shopping Center, Denver Nuggets and Colorado Music Educators Association have sponsored a competition for young musicians, 30 of whom are selected to perform at the mall in the Colorado Youth Pops Orchestra. Each member receives a $1,000 scholarship upon graduating from high school. The program also provides musical instruments to elementary school children.

From Central City Opera to the Denver Municipal Band, arts groups began a Community Awareness Partnership Residency at Highlands Ranch High School in 1995, with hands-on workshops teaching everything from vocal technique to "Business in the Entertainment World." The Denver Lyric Opera Guild and Young Musicians Foundation are among other groups helping to extend musical excellence into the next generation.

©PILON STUDIO OF PHOTOGRAPHY

Vincent C. LaGuardia Jr. of the Arapahoe Philharmonic Orchestra

THE BOULDER PHILHARMONIC ON STAGE AT MACKY
AUDITORIUM
© FOTO IMAGERY/TIM MURPHY

KEVIN JOHNSON, ASSISTANT PRINCIPAL CELLIST
WITH THE BOULDER PHILHARMONIC, TAKES TIME O
OF THE CLASSROOM CONCERT PROGRAM TO TALK
WITH YOUNG MUSIC LOVERS.
COURTESY OF THE BOULDER PHILHARMONIC

THE COLORADO WIND ENSEMBLE

© D.L.S. PHOTOGRAPHIC PRODUCTS AND SERVICES

JULIUS GLAIHENGAUZ
CONDUCTS A REHEARSAL OF
THE VERDI REQUIEM BY THE
CENTENNIAL PHILHARMONIC
AND THE COLORADO
MORMON CHORALE.
PHOTOS BY
ROBERT B. DALLENBACH

Hot Jam
by Jeff Bradley

Even if you've never been to Denver, you probably know about Red Rocks Amphitheatre, regularly voted the most popular concert venue in the country by rock's biggest stars. The Moody Blues recorded a best-selling album and video there with the Colorado Symphony; John Tesh made a TV special; Bonnie Raitt is a frequent visitor; and Bruce Springsteen broke a personal ban on outdoor concerts by singing at Red Rocks—and loved it.

COURTESY OF THE ARVADA CENTER FOR THE ARTS AND HUMANITIES

"We told him Red Rocks isn't outdoors, it's indoors without a roof," said Barry Fey, Denver's leading concert promoter. "God made it, which gives it a big edge over everything else."

Framed by 400-foot sandstone rocks, the 8,000-seat amphitheater under the stars offers the quintessential Colorado experience—proximity to the beauty and power of the mountains combined with the energy of a big city and the intimacy of a recital hall. Being in a Red Rocks crowd is about as close as you can get these days to experiencing the "peace and love" vibes of the '60s.

An extraordinary view of the Front Range mountains is also a feature of modern Fiddler's Green Amphitheatre in suburban Englewood. This much larger, 18,000-seat outdoor facility is where crowds gather to hear Elton John, Herbie Hancock or José Carreras.

For megastars such as the Rolling Stones, the Eagles and the Grateful Dead, bigger turnouts

BRINGING THE STARS CLOSER

Jeff Bradley

When Denver residents think of rock music, the first name that comes to mind is Barry Fey, promoter extraordinaire, the local equivalent to San Francisco's late Bill Graham. He is largely responsible for making Denver a "must" stop on every national tour.

"I've been a consistent voice here for 27 years as the music has developed, and I've always insisted on good sound, good lighting. All the acts rate Denver as the first or second best show on their tour.

"We have great facilities, whether it's Red Rocks, the Paramount, the Auditorium Theater or Macky Auditorium or, in the old days, the Rainbow and Ebbets Field. Led Zeppelin played their first date here on December 26, 1968. We had the last appearance of the Jimi Hendrix Experience on June 28, 1979, and we had one of the last appearances of Big Brother & the Holding Company. The best always comes to us."

are accommodated at the city's McNichols Sports Arena, home of the NBA Denver Nuggets; Mile-High Stadium, playground of John Elway of the Denver Broncos; or the Denver Performing Arts Complex.

Among Denver summer traditions, none is more popular than the annual series of concerts on the sunken stage of the Botanic Gardens, a haven of serenity in the heart of the city. Families arrive early to set up blankets on the sloping lawn and to dive into picnic baskets of Oriental chicken, arugula salad and fine wine. Many stroll around the fragrant roses, Japanese tea garden and exotic blooms before the show starts; you might see '60s pop singer Marianne Faithfull, the Chieftains from Ireland, the Cajun troupe Beausoleil, the Lincoln Center Jazz Orchestra or colorful African drummers.

Watching the sunset in such a sweet-scented environment creates a relaxed ambience. When contemporary balladeer Kenny Rankin was interrupted by heavy rain, members of the audience literally stood over him with their umbrellas so the show could go on. Folk singer Judy Collins, who grew up in Denver and produced an award-winning documentary about her old piano teacher Antonia Brico, used a Botanic Gardens concert to premiere a nostalgic song about being snowbound in Colorado.

Just off downtown Denver's 16th Street Mall is the historic Paramount Theatre, host to touring acts as big as Stevie Wonder or as fringe as performance artist Laurie Anderson. In recent years smaller theaters and clubs in Denver and Boulder have made it possible for alternative and emerging bands to find an audience. Big Head Todd and the Monsters came out of this scene.

Denver venues include the old Ogden and Bluebird theaters on Colfax Avenue, the city's neon east-west drag, as well as Herman's Hideaway rock club and the bohemian Mercury Cafe, which offers everything from a solo cello with Sunday brunch to ballroom dancing, acid rock and cutting-edge theater. At most of these places you can order a draft beer or a designer coffee and sit at a small table to enjoy the show.

One month's lineup at the Bluebird Theater gives a flavor of the diversity on tap: jazz saxophonist Joshua Redman; blues guitarist Jimmy Johnson; a $4 senior citizen screening of the movie *Damn Yankees*; the rap groups Lord of Word and the Disciples of Bass; an Israeli cabaret; a triple bill with rocker Mitch Ryder, jazz trumpeter Ron Miles and the world beat group Talking Drum; an AIDS benefit dance; and concerts by grunge rock and country western groups.

Arnold Schwarzenegger is among investors in Denver's booming Lower Downtown, a once-rundown warehouse district now home to brew-pubs, glitzy restaurants, galleries and lofts, with plenty of live music from acoustic rock to fusion.

Each summer the AT&T Wireless Services LoDo Music Festival fills the streets of LoDo near picturesque Union Station, where all Western railroads once stopped. Outdoor stages offer music for all tastes just a short walk from the new Coors Field, home of the National League's Colorado Rockies.

The Boulder scene is also prolific, thanks to the laid-back atmosphere of the Fox and Boulder theaters where performers have included k.d. lang, Arlo Guthrie, Junior Wells and Loreena McKennitt. The public radio show "E-Town" is taped each week at the funky Boulder Theater.

An outdoor-oriented college town whose institutions include the Buddhist Naropa Institute, Boulder is a haven for New Age music. Local composer Bill Douglas has gone skyward with his Hearts of Space recordings and collaborations with crossover clarinet virtuoso Richard Stoltzman.

The acoustic music revolution that ended rock's hold on the public in the late 1980s found fertile ground throughout Colorado, prompting the creation of groups like Wind Machine and the appearance of local recording studios and labels such as Boulder's Silver Wave Records.

This is the West, and for many country western is king—especially at the 4,000-square-foot Grizzly Rose Saloon and Dance Hall, recent winner of the Country Music Association's Nightclub of the Year Award and a required stop for such performers as Willie Nelson and Emmy Lou Harris.

Since half the fun is two-stepping on the huge dance floor, crowds arrive early to stake out a space—or take a lesson before the main event. The huge building includes billiards tables,

country boutiques and barrels of beer. Country dancing is also popular at the Cactus Moon Saloon in the northern suburb of Thornton.

By the way, among Denver's many oldies, rock, jazz, classical and talk radio stations, country music's KYGO consistently tops local ratings.

HAPPENIN' DENVER

Jeff Bradley

Ellyn Rucker is one of many highly talented jazz musicians who'd rather be in Denver than battling for recognition in New York or Los Angeles. Originally from Des Moines, Iowa, the versatile jazz pianist and singer came to Denver in 1957 and, despite spells of performing elsewhere, decided to stay. Owner of a beautiful little house in North Denver, she keeps busy at local clubs and festivals.

"First of all, it's a really beautiful place to live. It's got the climate and a lot to offer from the personal lifestyle point of view. There's a wonderful ethnicity which broadens our cultural scope—a great mix of things with an infusion from both the black and Hispanic communities and a lot of crossover. There're sports, there's music, there's an abundance of social situations people can take part in, and there's all this great scenery.

"If you can't find anything to do in Denver, you're not awake. We've got 2 million people in this city. Denver is happening. But it's also a city where you can maneuver economically and time-wise—you can be across town in 20 minutes. You can actually own a house here. You can feel your way around a city this size. We're getting some good recording studios in the area as well. If the economy holds, I think we can expect even more great things.

"I also think we probably have as many good playing opportunities, if not more, than in any other city. It would be monstrous to try to carve out a living playing music in New York City today.

"We have a wonderful jazz station 24 hours a day [KUVO-FM], which is hard to find in other cities. True, there aren't enough real jazz clubs for the number of musicians we have, though we do have some crossover clubs and a lot of fusion. But there is diversity and I just love that about Denver. I've been out on the road and can compare. Denver is still my first choice as a place to live and work."

Like Red Rocks, singer Lannie Garrett is a Denver institution. She's been entertaining audiences here for two decades with her tongue-in-cheek Patsy DeCline country show, torchy nightclub act, big band spectacular or Colorado Symphony pops.

For those who like to play, not just watch, Swallow Hill Music Hall offers instruction in picking the banjo, slamming the conga or singing the country blues. It's a down-home kind of place that sometimes spills over into neighboring Cameron Church for intimate concerts by local standouts such as Carla Sciaky and Mary

TOP: Red Rocks Amphithe-atre is carved out of 400-foot-high boulders.
BOTTOM: A zesty flair fills the streets at the annual Cinco de Mayo festival.

Flower. Open stage nights at Swallow Hill and local coffee bars provide singers, songwriters and pickers a first hearing, while Swallow Hill also sponsors concerts by big names such as Tom Paxton. Each spring a dozen of Denver's finest female folkies tour the Front Range in a collegial group they call The Mother Folkers, a tongue-in-cheek but talented ensemble that's outlived musical fads and survived the coming and going of new members. Their loyal following is legion.

Whether local R&B stalwart Hazel Miller or the area's growing number of harmony-crazed a cappella singing groups, acts of all kinds get a chance to perform at the Capitol Hill People's Fair and the Festival of Mountain and Plain: A Taste of Colorado, both held in Civic Center Park each summer, as well as at downtown's alcohol-free First Night Colorado on New Year's Eve.

In the Hispanic quarter just west of downtown, Santa Fe Drive is transformed for the Cinco de Mayo celebration that includes the hottest salsa and mariachi bands around. El Noa Noa is the best of several Mexican restaurants along the strip. There's more outdoor music on multiple stages at the Cherry Creek Arts Festival each July as well as at the Denver Black Arts Festival in City Park, the annual Japanese Cherry Blossom Festival at Sakura Square and the pilsner-drenched Oktoberfest downtown.

Overall, this energized pop music scene entertains and chronicles life in a town where the median age is in the low 30s.

Denver has enjoyed a vibrant jazz scene since African-American violinist George Morrison (1891-1974) led a dance band before and after World War I. Morrison's long career paralleled the development of jazz and popular music, and he indirectly helped a number of big names get started. Despite classical training and free lessons with Fritz Kreisler, who was greatly impressed by his playing, Morrison couldn't build a career on the concert platform because of his color.

A contractual dispute also prevented him from accepting an offer to record for the Victor label in 1920. Instead, he recommended a white musician who'd been his fellow student in Denver—Paul Whiteman, son of Wilberforce Whiteman, head of music instruction in Denver's public schools. The young Whiteman was locked in the family sewing room when he balked at practicing the violin, but the discipline paid off. At the age of 17 he joined the Denver Symphony viola section, later advancing to the San Francisco Symphony.

After Morrison's introduction, Whiteman formed an orchestra and before long was billed as the "King of Jazz," making the country's new syncopated music respectable and presenting the 1924 world premiere of George Gershwin's *Rhapsody in Blue*. Meanwhile, Morrison played on the first blues record ever made, featuring singer Mamie Smith. He also invited Jimmy Lunceford, Andy Kirk and Jelly Roll Morton into his Denver band, along with singer Hattie McDaniel. All became stars.

By the 1940s Denver had a bustling black community centered on the Five Points district where Duke Ellington, Count Basie, Lena Horne, Art Tatum, Dizzy Gillespie and Lionel Hampton came to perform. With men pouring into local army and air bases, the Casino Ballroom, Rossonian Hotel, Voters' Club, Ex-Servicemen's Club and other joints made Five Points a mecca for jazz and nightlife. Local session players included the great Paul Quinichette on sax.

While these legendary clubs have all closed and the Five Points neighborhood declined, Denver has retained its appetite for good jazz.

Investment banker Dick Gibson invented the "jazz party" in 1963 and ran it every Labor Day weekend for 30 years in Denver, Colorado Springs or Aspen. In the process he helped keep jazz alive at a time when the nation's musical pulse switched to rock.

Gibson, who still presents jazz every week on the radio, also staged an annual series of jam sessions at the Paramount Theatre, mixing swing and bop musicians with surprising results. Audiences became accustomed to seeing Benny Carter, Milt Hinton, Harry "Sweets" Edison, Buddy De Franco, Phil Woods and other legendary performers.

These days crowds catch the same breed of players at the Park Hill Golf Club supper club in concerts often built around stride pianist Ralph Sutton, who lives in the mountains west of Denver. One recent lineup included bassist Ray Brown with Milt Jackson on vibes and Cedar Walton on piano.

Each fall lovers of traditional New Orleans jazz gather at a Denver Tech Center hotel for the Summit Jazz Festival to march down Rampart Street with the Jim Cullum Jazz Band and other trad jazz groups.

With its noisy neighborhood bar atmosphere and Mexican menu, El Chapultepec remains the city's most eclectic jazz bar, serving up elbow-rubbing camaraderie and big-name special guests. More upscale, the Vartan Jazz Club in posh Cherry Creek showcases both local talent and stars such as Roy Hargrove, Eddie Gomez and James Moody. Not even in New York can you find such a reverential atmosphere for jazz: owner Vartan Tonoian insists on no talking or clattering during performances, a mural on the wall honors the legendary jazz musicians and there's a state-of-the-art sound system for recordings and relays on local jazz station KUVO.

Dozens of restaurants, clubs and coffee bars offer live jazz, while host Kenny Burgmaier's local *Jazz Alley* TV program is nationally syndicated.

One of the newest jazz spots is Pasta Jay's restaurant on Market Street in LoDo, where "Pasta Jazz on the Roof" on Thursday nights presents the area's best players, many of whom have toured nationally but choose to live along the Front Range. They include pianists Eric Gunnison (Carmen McRae's former accompanist), Art Lande and Ellyn Rucker; trumpeter Ron Miles; saxophonist Nelson Rangell; bassists Kenny Walker and Paul Warburton; and guitarist Dale Bruning. Boulder produced noted tenor saxophonist Spike Robinson, while pianist Dave Grusin and his brother Don grew up in the southern suburb of Littleton.

Tax money makes it possible for Creative Music Works and the Colorado New Music Association to stretch listeners' ears with avant-garde jazz from artists such as Anthony Braxton, Marilyn Crispell and composer/saxophonist Fred Hess.

For lifestyle and musical reasons, the trend in recent years is for jazz artists (including singer Dianne Reeves, who grew up in Denver) to leave Los Angeles and New York and settle down in Denver, a very musical city.

ELLYN RUCKER
COURTESY OF ELLYN RUCKER

THE DENVER BRASS

THE DENVER BRASS IN CONCERT AT THE MCI BUILDING, 1993
COURTESY OF THE DENVER BRASS

Perceptions of Denver
by Jane Fudge

Like the rivers that made young Denver's growth possible, the rich cultural current that originated with Colorado's land and native peoples joined with streams of 19th-century settlers that poured into the Front Range from every part of the country. The arts and crafts the newcomers brought with them, commingled with the established traditions of the longtime inhabitants, endowed the raw towns of the Front Range with a welcome sense of permanence. Today the visual arts and artists of Denver and its Front Range neighbors are as diverse and imaginative as their history would suggest.

"ABACUS SLIDING" BY SAM GILLIAM, 1977,
POLYMER PIGMENT ON CANVAS
COURTESY OF THE DENVER ART MUSEUM

Metropolitan Denver is the most isolated large city in the 48 contiguous states, but it is as vital a national nerve center in the era of flight and electronics as it was in railroad and telegraph days. Artists here have developed a sturdy independence from the trends of the coastal art centers, while taking advantage of a constant exchange of information about ideas and issues from afar. Yet the youthfulness of Colorado's institutions, the Western folklore of innocence and individualism, even the sublime topography itself, lend the arts a certain vulnerability. They cannot be properly described in glib terms like "regionalism"; contrary to Denver and environs being a definable "region," the artistic community is essentially without a geographic center.

ABOVE: **"Obstacles in My Way" by Gloria Vialpando** RIGHT: **The Mackey Gallery** BOTTOM: **"Boy and Frog" by Elsie Ward Haring, from the Collection of the City and County of Denver**

© MARY MACKEY 1993

PHOTO BY GREG ESSER

There is no SoHo, no North Beach, no Montmartre. That frees Denver's artists from orthodoxy, but it makes their work difficult to define—a mixed blessing, for labels are the common stock of art criticism and history.

However, scores of artists continue to come here, for reasons as diverse as their work. Some are attracted by the special quality of the light, others are inspired by the landscape, and still others like the sense of freedom and opportunity that living and working in a relatively young city imparts. Those who leave often return; Denver's visual arts community boasts a surprising continuity and many artists who enjoy international reputations make their homes here. Denver's artists look not only to galleries, museums and cultural institutions for affirmation but also to each other.

Basic public support is provided to artists and arts organizations by such agencies as the Mayor's Office of Art, Culture and Film (MOACF), the state-supported Colorado Council on the Arts and numerous local arts councils. A great demand exists for assistance from these groups, which provide reliable funding for such vital services as the Colorado Artists Register. CAR provides slides and computerized information about more than 1,600 of the state's professional artists to curators, architects and collectors—at no charge to either the users or the artists. The MOACF also has an artist registry that is widely used.

Other organizations focus their attention on particular groups, like the Rocky Mountain Women's Institute, whose associateships include a studio, administrative support and a small stipend. Visual arts associates of RMWI meet regularly with associates who are writers and scholars, and all present their work at the Institute's annual Associate Showcase. Another success story is the Chicano Humanities and Arts Council, a cultural fixture in predominantly Hispanic northwest Denver. It mounts exhibitions, creates neighborhood art programs and has encouraged the work of Hispanic artists since the early 1980s.

Denver artists and gallery owners have discovered the strength that lies in numbers, banding together not only for moral but practical support as well. Leaving rugged individualism to the studio, they blend business acumen with creativity to share information, publicity and other services. Practically every gallery, from smartly appointed spaces in upmarket Cherry Creek North and Boulder to the clusters of galleries in LoDo to the cheerfully anarchic co-ops, has joined others to capture new and larger audiences.

In the city center, more than 30 retail galleries belong to the Lower Downtown Arts District. A couple of blocks near Wazee and 17th streets are home to the venerable contemporary galleries, Robischon Gallery and Sandy Carson. Neighbors include such specialists as Sloane Gallery, which shows contemporary Russian art; The Art of Craft; and 1/1 (One Over One), which has prints and monotypes in profusion. Metropolitan State College of Denver's Center for Visual Arts gallery—off campus and about as far from "academic" as one can imagine—

© ROBERT ADAMS

ROBERT ADAMS

Jane Fudge

For more than 30 years, photographer Robert Adams has lived and worked in Boulder County, making photographs that show the beauty and fragility of the Western landscape, that delicate and ragged interface where nature and human development meet. Adams' work is widely honored. He has had two John Simon Guggenheim Memorial Foundation fellowships and in 1994 was one of 20 recipients of the new "genius grants" from the John D. and Catherine T. MacArthur Foundation. Though Adams holds a doctorate in English literature, he turned to photography in 1970 to express the impact of expanding population on ecology.

Since then he has published more than a dozen books and his photographs are in the permanent collections of the Museum of Modern Art, the Metropolitan Museum of Art in New York and many European museums. Closer to home, Adams has had four exhibitions at the Denver Art Museum, which owns three complete Adams series, *Prairie*, *From the Missouri West* and *Summer Nights*. A touring retrospective of his photography was seen at the Colorado History Museum in 1990. "I want to make accurate photographs of the Western landscape," Adams says, "to show what's wrong so we'll change it." Another goal, he adds, "is to show what's right and take some hope in it."

"Poplar Trees, Longmont," part of the
Summer Nights series by Robert Adams.
Collection Denver Art Museum
Gift of Elizabeth B. Shwayder

puts on avant-garde shows in a corner space. Nearby at CSK Gallery, fine prints, most created by local artists, are produced, shown and sold. Within walking distance are Grant Gallery on Market Street, showing contemporary and vintage photography; and Rule Modern and Contemporary, a showroom space in the renovated Ice House, near Union Station. First Friday

events, held monthly when exhibitions change, attract throngs of art lovers, flowing from gallery to gallery and in and out of the district's restaurants and nightclubs.

In contrast, Denver's numerous—and durable—cooperative galleries stay open on shoestring budgets. They, too, have an "umbrella" organization, the Alternative Arts

SOMEWHERE BETWEEN FLORENCE AND DENVER

Jane Fudge

Travelers hurrying across the bridge spanning Denver International Airport's main terminal pass the colorful ceramic balustrade created by Betty Woodman, a Boulder-based artist who maintains studios in New York City and Florence, Italy, with her husband, painter and photographer George Woodman. The two met when Betty was teaching a ceramics class at Harvard, and in 1957 they moved to Boulder, where both now teach in the Fine Arts Department of the University of Colorado. All along Betty produced handsome, marketable pottery but became more and more interested in non-functional pieces derived from vessel forms; for example, elegantly decorated but outsized pitchers or platters.

"Diana," 1991 by Betty Woodman
COURTESY OF THE DENVER ART MUSEUM

In 1980 the pair took spaces in New York, where George prepared for a show of his jigsaw-like "pattern" paintings at the Guggenheim Museum. But working in three different places made it clear to Betty that she could not maintain two distinct types of ceramics. "I gave up pots," she says. Pots or sculpture, Betty Woodman's work—much of it complete environments in glazed ceramic—has found enthusiastic audiences in the United States, Europe and Japan. Two of her vases are on display in the lobby of the Museum of Modern Art in New York, and her flamboyant diptych "Diana" is in the Denver Art Museum's permanent collection. Meanwhile, George's graceful and intricate painting led him from canvas to paper tile to the real thing: an interlace of floral or figurative images superimposed on the grid of ceramic tile. He continues to paint and make haunting photographs but has executed several public commissions in tile. One of his most recent is displayed in the ceramic lobby wall of the Temple Hoyne Buell Theatre in the recently renovated Denver Performing Arts Complex. Ceramic Woodmans can now greet visitors at the DIA or delight the eyes of theater patrons between the acts downtown.

Alliance, which has represented them since 1986. Current members include Pirate, Spark, CORE, Asylum, ZIP37 and Edge, all organized since the 1970s, and Off Center Gallery, Genre, Ulozi and Ec-Lec-Tic Art. Co-op gallery "crawls" can be time-consuming, for the spaces are scattered throughout Denver and its suburbs, though most are in the northwest Denver renaissance area near Mackey Gallery and the Chicano Humanities and Arts Council.

Imagination welded to pragmatism forms the armature on which Denver's arts community is built. Monumental sculpture is one of the most difficult idioms to present to an audience, so for the past 10 years sculptor Robert Mangold and his wife, Peggy, have operated Artyard, an outdoor showplace on Denver's South Pearl Street.

Denver artists combine tenacity and optimism with creativity to not only survive in this sometimes unpredictable cultural upland but to prevail.

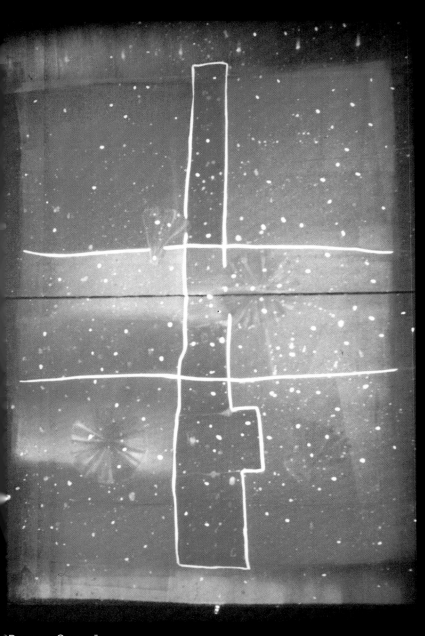

"BROKEN CROSS"

BY GLORIA VIALPANDO

"CARNIVAL WHEEL AT NIGHT, LONGMONT"
FROM ROBERT ADAMS' *SUMMER NIGHTS* SERIES.
COLLECTION DENVER ART MUSEUM

"SELF"
BY R. EDWARD LOWE

"SELF" (DETAIL)

BY R. EDWARD LOWE

Art in Public Places
by Jane Fudge

In the first decade of the 20th century, Denverites reflected upon their city's hasty and drab appearance. Under flamboyant political boss Mayor Robert Speer, and subsequent city fathers and mothers, Denver invented itself as the "City Beautiful" with new parks and public buildings graced with sculpture and paintings. Through several early programs—including one with the questionable title "Give While You Live"—Denver got many of its best-loved landmarks, like Mabel Landrum Torrey's "Wynken, Blynken and Nod," now in Washington Park, and "Broncho Buster" by Alexander Phimister Proctor at Civic Center Park. However, popular support for works of art in public places was inconstant, rising and falling with the city's fortunes.

"STUDIO VIEWS"
BY SUSAN COOPER, 66"x98"x18"
ARTIST'S COLLECTION

In the 1960s the City Beautiful spirit was reborn in historic preservation and beautification efforts. At the same time, modernist trends in art, which had developed while Denver's arts were in a period of quiescence, sometimes made projects controversial.

Paradoxically, early signs of renewal in the public arts often came from private interest groups. The Friends of Contemporary Art accomplished the siting of several large, abstract outdoor sculptures at Burns Park in the city's southeast quadrant in the 1970s. Other corporate and citizen art-lovers founded the Denver Sculpture Committee and made possible Denver's unique "Solar Fountain" by Larry Bell and Eric Orr.

Energy booms in the '70s and '80s attracted a legion of businesses to Denver. These newcomers moved into freshly built skyscrapers and proclaimed their tastes and cultural identities with works of art in lobbies and plazas all over town. Abstract sculpture by Steven Antonakis, Harry Bertoia, Denverite Robert Mangold, Robert Behrens and Kenneth Snelson sprouted in the granite and concrete prairies of downtown real estate, and corporate collections blossomed on the walls of banks, exploration companies and law offices. Today shopping meccas such as

ABOVE: **The Sullivan Gate at Denver City Park**
RIGHT: **"The Old Prospector" is edged into place at the Mining Exchange Building.**
FAR RIGHT: **Kit Carson sits atop Frederick MacMonnies' Pioneer Fountain**

Cherry Creek North make room for outdoor sculpture; even the Regional Transportation District, which operates metropolitan-area buses and light rail, places borrowed works at its shuttle terminal for passersby to admire. The yellow corkscrew of "Articulated Wall," a masterwork of the late Bauhaus artist and longtime Colorado resident Herbert Bayer, pins down the asphalt ribbons of intersecting South Broadway and Interstate 25.

Suburban Englewood prizes its Museum of Outdoor Arts, a 400-acre suburban business park in Greenwood Plaza dotted with outdoor sculpture ranging from Harry Marinsky's life-sized "Mad Tea Party," complete with sleepy dormouse, to the shining wheel of Arnaldo Pomodoro's "Disco Emergente."

Until fairly recently, however, publicly funded programs to buy and preserve artworks were sporadic if enthusiastic. The state Public Art Program, administered by Colorado Council on the Arts, began placing contemporary work at university campuses and public buildings—even prisons—in the early 1980s. Since then CCA has made scores of commissions and direct purchases statewide, and acquisitions range from paintings and drawings to site-specific, complex installations such as Dale Eldred's 1994 "Light + Time Labyrinth" at the Auraria Higher Education Center in Denver.

Denver once had several public arts advisory councils, with overlapping and sometimes competing responsibilities. During the tenure of Mayor Federico Peña, their duties were consolidated in the Commission on Cultural Affairs, now, under Mayor Wellington E. Webb, the Denver Mayor's Commission on Art, Culture and Film (MCACF); an executive order signed in 1988 by Mayor Peña established Denver's public art program. City Hall's encouragement of the arts was furthered during the administration of Mayor Webb, who led the effort to make the public art program permanent through the passage of a new law, causing public projects to flourish throughout the city. For any new public

construction and rehabilitation projects of $1 million or more, one percent of the total cost must be set aside to commission or acquire works of art.

This reliable source of funds has had a dramatic effect on Denver's public face, with more than 40 new works of art since 1988. Murals and friezes enliven the tunnels and street improve-

ART IN THE SERVICE OF HARMONY
Jane Fudge

Leo Tanguma, who moved from his native Texas to Denver in 1983, is a muralist who regularly works with volunteers, often children, from the neighborhoods in which he creates his paintings. Tanguma's work is characterized by a commitment to the power of art to effect social change. More than 17 of his murals exist in and around Houston, Texas, and he has major works in Denver, Seattle and Chicago. Tanguma has received many awards both for his art and for his dedication to each community in which he has lived, and although most of Tanguma's paintings are permanent installations, his work was included in the national traveling exhibition *Chicano Art, Resistance and Affirmation*. In 1989 his freestanding "sculptural mural," "La Antorcha de Quetzalcoatl," commissioned by the Denver Art Museum, was shown at several Colorado and New Mexico museums.

Leo Tanguma's monumental commission for Denver International Airport is "The Children of the World Dream of Peace," which contrasts harmonious relationships between humankind and nature with the negative impact on nature of heedless development and a short-term material gain. Part of the Collection of the City and County of Denver, the brilliantly colored mural shows children from around the world in festive folk dress converging on the glowing image of an endangered rain forest orchid. A Mexican girl in a flowing skirt dances with a crane, while other children, their faces reflecting dismay and horror, discover the carcass of the nearly extinct snow leopard. Tanguma says that he wants travelers passing through DIA to "see themselves depicted with beauty and dignity, in the greatest quest of all—to live in peace with one another."

ments that crisscross a revitalized Platte Valley. The tiered-glass entryway to the Colorado Convention Center blazes like a gargantuan jeweler's case with the dancing reflections from Steven DeVries' soaring prismatic sculpture "Temporal Speculation," while on exterior walls Barbara Jo Revelle's digitized photographic

ART TAKES OFF AT DIA

Jane Fudge

When Denverites voted to build a new airport, they also opted for what amounted to a sizeable museum of public art projects that used the talents of 42 artists from Denver and elsewhere in the country. The public art portion of Denver International's total projected budget mandated by city ordinance amounted to $7.5 million and was administered by the Denver Mayor's Office of Art, Culture and Film, under the direction of Joyce Oberfeld. A DIA art steering committee, advisory committee, design team and a host of selection panelists met for months to address the myriad issues that surround placing works of art in an airport's heavily used public spaces. Artists were encouraged to consider collaborative works and to integrate their pieces into the actual fabric of the buildings. The artworks of DIA are no afterthought.

The variety of subjects, media and styles of work throughout DIA is astonishing. There are colorful representational paintings by Navajo artist Allen Mose and Chicano artist-activist Leo Tanguma, and bronze figurative sculptures by Ed Dwight and George Lundeen, whose piece was donated by the Jeppeson Foundation. The automated trains that whisk passengers to the outlying concourses announce their arrival with Jim Green's "sound sculpture," an electronic chime that whimsically plays "She'll Be Comin' 'Round the Mountain." Once under way, the trains flash past lighted installations in their subterranean tunnels. Wall-mounted propellers by the artist team of Antonette Rosato and William Maxwell whirl in the draft of the passing cars. "Deep Time, Deep Space—A Subterranean Journey" by Leni Schwendinger is a mile of Colorado history told in shimmering, fleeting images. There is vaulting environmental sculpture by David Griggs at the center of Concourse A, and a glass canopy by Alice Adams in Concourse B. A squadron of gaily painted metal "paper airplanes" by Patty Ortiz points the way from the shuttle platform to the main terminal, and Doug Hollis' "Mountain Mirage" replicates the famed silhouette of the Rocky Mountains in water. Some DIA pieces reflect the humor that is sometimes required of travelers: The hunkering bronze gargoyles of Terry Allen's "Notre Denver" preside over the baggage claim. And just in case you want to make a last-minute change of destination, Gary Sweeney's "America, Why I Love Her" map offers such attractions as Ashburn, Georgia, home of the world's largest peanut. What better reason could there be for a detour?

mural rendered in tile depicts the many faces and races who have made Colorado history. Susan Cooper's vivid new relief cityscapes nestle as comfortably in their niches in the rotunda of City and County Building as the painted murals of her predecessor, Allen Tupper True, have done in their neoclassical Civic Center Park settings since the 1930s and 1940s. MOACF's biggest triumph to date, however, is Denver International Airport. DIA's art program alone constitutes enough sculpture, painting, photography, installations and architectural members to handsomely adorn a small municipality.

Denver's many works of art on public view have endured periods of neglect, even abuse and loss. Taking heed of the area's cultural legacy, preservationist groups such as Historic Denver and The Parks People have set about to raise

money to restore damaged or endangered public paintings and sculptures. A push is under way to ensure that new publicly funded projects have conservation and maintenance funds built in.

COURTESY OF DIA

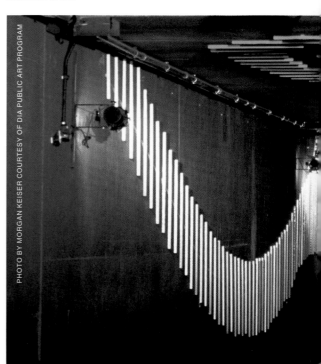

PHOTO BY MORGAN KEISER COURTESY OF DIA PUBLIC ART PROGRAM

In 1994 the Denver chapter of Save Outdoor Sculpture!, a national program sponsored by the Smithsonian Institution and the National Institute for the Conservation of Cultural Property, completed a yearlong effort dedicated to locating and logging all such works on a national database. SOS! Denver, based at the Fine Arts Department of the University of Colorado at Denver, gathered research about more than 150 sculptures in the metro area and held a public art symposium that kicked off the statewide undertaking, Colorado SOS!

The City and County of Denver, realizing the value and investment in public art, has formed an interagency maintenance task force that oversees the maintenance of artwork in the city's col-

lection. Relying heavily on the expert opinions of arts and conservator professionals, each agency contributes funds to the effort. One of the task force's initiatives, Adopt an Artwork, attempts to identify public or private sources of additional funds for restoration of art works in the collection.

At the turn of another new century, the heritage of the City Beautiful is carried on in dozens of privately and publicly supported art projects—enduring evidence of the region's wealth of artistic styles, materials and meanings.

These pieces are from the Collection of the City and County of Denver.
ABOVE: "Colorado Panorama: A People's History" (detail) by Barbara Jo Revelle is a series of photographs translated to tile.
INSET UPPER LEFT: "Notre Denver" (detail) by Terry Allen
LEFT: "Deep Time, Deep Space—A Subterranean Journey" by Leni Schwendinger

HISTORICAL LANDSCAPE

Molly Squibb and the Denver Public Library

"A rolling historical landscape" is how artist Edward Ruscha describes his panoramic artwork for the Central Library. The work unfolds in epic fashion on 70 painted panels high above Schlessman Hall and in the atriums on either side of the hall.

Ruscha is world renowned for his ability to mix words and images in a masterful counterpoint of reality and illusion. For the Central Library,

he has silhouetted familiar icons in twilight landscapes, enhancing the mythic quality of America's westward migration. The artist's medium is acrylic color, applied by airbrush for a strokeless, smoky effect.

The complete artwork took more than two years to complete from concept to finished canvas. It was commissioned by the Denver Mayor's Commission on Art, Culture and Film, which awards one percent of major public construction budgets for original art. A panel of local art and design professionals selected Ruscha's entry from more than 420 submissions in a national competition.

SCHLESSMAN HALL

Perhaps you're asking, "Where do I start?" Begin anywhere, the artist suggests, but be sure to walk the distance. The flow of the work is enforced by the east-west axis of magnificent Schlessman Hall, hub of the Central Library. At the east end, the sun rises over images of wagon and railroad trains that span the length of the hall on facing panels. Both caravans are heading westward into the afterglow of a sunset.

"The 360-degree panorama compresses within its 'day' a metaphor for the beginnings of Denver history," the artist explains. "It was important for these paintings to become brothers and sisters to each other, to relate, yet to be independent."

THE ATRIUMS

In the east and west atriums, the historic migration is punctuated by icons ("suggesters," in Ruscha's words) of the Old West: Native American tepees; a gold rush pick, pan and shovel; the Colorado lark bunting; a buffalo. Here the artist's focus broadens to include thought-provoking images of the earth and the universe beyond. Painted subjects hint at the rich lode of information found in a public library: science, geography, astronomy and communications. Open dictionaries suggest the alphabet from A to Z in east and west panels.

"East to West, A to Z, sunrise to sunset," the artist says. "The Library encompasses a base for human experience, knowledge and all thought worthy of words and books." Each panel can also be viewed as "a random painting. Viewers will see what they want in them, as they should," adds the artist, who nevertheless has placed some clues to his own vision . . .

THE EAST ATRIUM

Anamorphic writing: In the tepee paintings, famous names from Native American history appear in letters so elongated they can barely

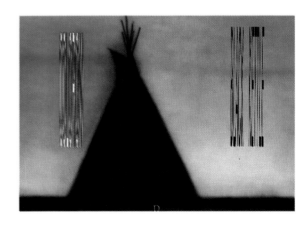

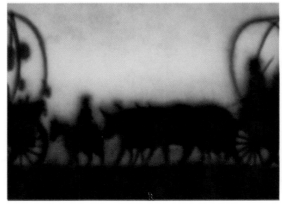

be read from a distance. The artist points out that this technique of optical distortion has been used for centuries. Step closer beneath the words (on the ground floor), look up and the foreshortened letters of Colorado native names—Ouray, Ute, Jack, Colorow, Black Kettle and Chipeta, wife of Chief Ouray—become legible.

Voice prints: "They came about by accident," admits the artist. "Reading the history of Colorado natives made me think of voices from the past. The use of anamorphics planted a vertical motion in my mind, and voice prints evolved into acoustically vertical images." The buffalo panel voice prints bring to life a second and a half of a stampede and the beast's snorts and sneezes. The trill of the lark bunting accents the painting of the Colorado state bird. For additional prints, the artist's wife read selected words aloud, which were then transposed, via computer, into graphic prints.

South Pole panel: This glance at the Earth's southern hemisphere is a geographical reference the artist found appropriate to a public library. What about the deep green splash that appears to slide off the panel? "My thinking drifted to ancient mariners, who believed land masses would fall off the bottom of the world if it were round," Ruscha says.

THE WEST ATRIUM

Communication (south side): Includes references to the early telegraph, a city postmark and 19th-century Denver's silver tongued huckster, Soapy Smith.

Shooting Stars (east): "The viewer can see

this as snowflakes, cosmic star patterns, a school of diving fish or even a shower of coins that suggest the Denver Mint. The painted white dots are life-sized images of pennies, nickels, dimes and quarters," Ruscha says.

Encyclopedic Vision (east): The artist re-creates "a familiar diagram of how vision occurs, as the retina turns the image upside down in the eye."

INSTALLING THE ARTWORK

Edward Ruscha painted the 130-yard artwork on individual canvas panels in three separate studio locations: one for painting, the other two for viewing and preparation. The project was first measured out in the only space big enough—a parking lot next door. In June 1995 he shipped the finished paintings to Denver, where the cotton-canvas panels were hoisted into place. The six-day installation took place at night, while the Library was closed.

ABOUT THE ARTIST

Art critics worldwide consider Edward Ruscha to be an important painter and interpreter of popular American culture. His genius for raising common questions about words and imagery to a new level of expression has earned him a place in the history of 20th-century art.

The artist was born in Omaha, Nebraska, in 1937 and was raised in Oklahoma City. He studied painting at Chouinard Art Institute in Los Angeles. His early paintings of the Hollywood sign, Standard Oil gas stations and other contemporary icons of America thrust him into the national spotlight in the early 1960s.

Lately, Ruscha has become intrigued by popular images and characters of the Old West. The Denver Central Library artwork "contains many images I've used in smaller previous paintings, like birds, the buffalo, the wagon train, and the pick, pan and shovel," he says. "While I was painting [the panels], I kept thinking back to the Oklahoma Land Run mural I did on the school wall in the third grade. The Library paintings are the natural evolution of my work. Most of my art has addressed myself and my own private struggles. This project has given me an opportunity I seldom get to address the broader public." The artist also created a celebrated series of murals for Miami-Dade Public Library in 1985.

AMERICA

GREAT BIG COLD COUNTRY TO THE NORTH

WARM TROPICAL COUNTRY TO THE SOUTH

...WHY I LOVE HER

"AMERICA, WHY I LOVE HER"
BY GARY SWEENEY

"WYNKEN, BLYNKEN AND NOD"
BY MABEL LANDRUM TORREY
PHOTO BY WENDY HEISTERKAMP
COURTESY OF THE DENVER MAYOR'S
OFFICE OF ART, CULTURE AND FILM

METEORITE
FOUND NEAR CANYON DIABLO
WEIGHT 535 LBS.

MY SISTER GAIL
VACATION - 1962
(ACTUAL SIZE!)

Gary Sweeney

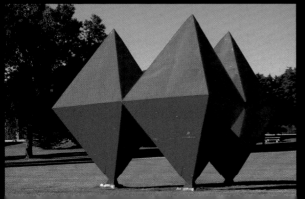

SCULPTURE BY ROGER KOTOSKE IN
BURNS PARK
PHOTO BY DAVID T. MACFARLANE JR.
COURTESY OF THE DENVER MAYOR'S
OFFICE OF ART, CULTURE AND FILM

THESE PIECES ARE PART OF THE
COLLECTION OF THE CITY AND COUNTY
OF DENVER

"Beginning a Century" (detail) from the
20th Century Perspectives collection
by Susan Cooper. Part of the Collection
of the City and County of Denver.
courtesy of the Denver Mayor's office
of Art, Culture and Film

"Matron of the High Plains" by Jennifer O'Meara

"Ending a Millenium" (detail) from the
20th Century Perspectives collection
by Susan Cooper. Part of the Collection of
the City and County of Denver.
courtesy of the Denver Mayor's office
of Art, Culture and Film

"BRONCHO BUSTER" BY
ALEXANDER PHIMISTER PROCTOR,
PART OF THE COLLECTION OF THE
CITY AND COUNTY OF DENVER
COURTESY OF DENVER METRO
CONVENTION & VISITORS BUREAU

THESE PIECES ARE PART OF THE COLLECTION OF THE CITY AND
COUNTY OF DENVER. TOP: "COLORADO VACATIONLAND" BY GARY
SWEENEY, 1992, OF PHOTOS, STEEL, BRONZE, WOOD AND NEON.
LEFT: "PETROS" BY BILL GIAN. PHOTO BY GREG ESSER
COURTESY OF DENVER MAYOR'S OFFICE OF ART, CULTURE AND FILM
ABOVE: "BRIDGE OF RECYCLING FOUNTAINS" BY LAURA AUDREY
COURTESY OF DENVER MAYOR'S OFFICE OF ART, CULTURE AND FILM

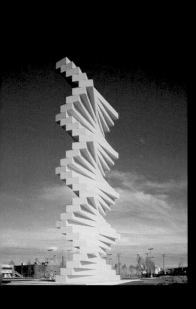

UPPER LEFT: "ARTICULATED WALL" BY HERBERT BAYER COURTESY OF THE DENVER ART MUSEUM

LOWER LEFT AND RIGHT: THESE PIECES ARE PART OF THE COLLECTION OF THE CITY AND COUNTY OF DENVER

"HUNGARIAN FREEDOM PARK MONUMENT" BY STEPHEN AND ZOLTAN POPOVITS

AND "FLAME OF COMPASSION" BY ROSS BARRABLE

PHOTOS COURTESY OF DENVER MAYOR'S OFFICE OF ART, CULTURE AND FILM

Who We Are
by Jane Fudge

Living in a metropolis young even by American standards, Denverites have always felt a special obligation to enshrine their brief past. Although its museums never enjoyed the extravagant patronage of the East, Denver built them with conviction and foresight. An embryonic Colorado Historical Society, Denver Art Museum and Denver Museum of Natural History were all in existence by 1900.

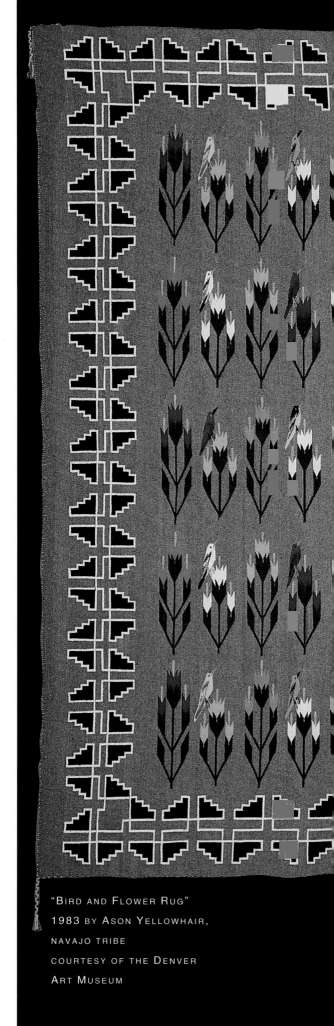

"BIRD AND FLOWER RUG"
1983 BY ASON YELLOWHAIR,
NAVAJO TRIBE
COURTESY OF THE DENVER
ART MUSEUM

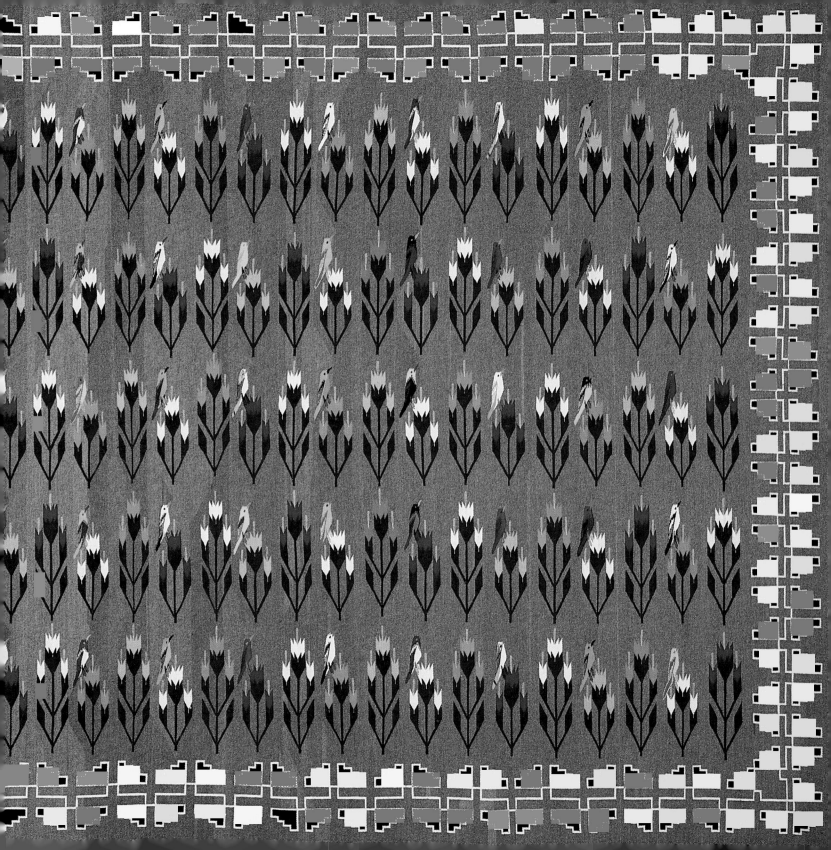

"Sky/Water," by Denverite R. Edward Lowe, featured a spectral canoe that sailed over visitors' heads and contained holographic images of clouds.

The Colorado History Museum, which grew out of a cheerfully elitist "pioneers" organization in 1879, now houses the huge and splendidly varied collections of artifacts, photographs, books, artworks and memorabilia of the state Historical Society. It lies, literally, within a stone's throw of the Central Library of the Denver Public Library and the Denver Art Museum.

These three are the centerpiece of the developing Civic Center Culture Complex; the History Museum is actually the flagship of a fleet of house museums and study centers scattered throughout the state. In addition to frequently changing exhibitions that document Colorado's yesterdays, the Museum presents the works of distinguished living artists such as photographer

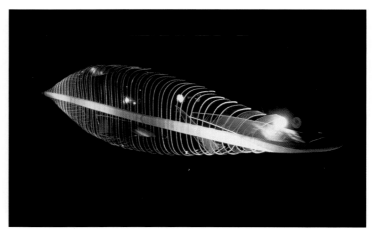

COURTESY R. EDWARD LOWE

AT CLOSE RANGE

Jane Fudge

A special feature of the Denver Art Museum's Modern and Contemporary Art galleries, "Close Range" has featured holographic installations and "sound" art and video, in addition to paintings, drawings, sculpture and photography. Though DAM sponsored annual contemporary shows for decades, collecting and showing work on art's cutting edge began in earnest in 1978, when Dianne Perry Vanderlip was hired as the Museum's first curator of contemporary art.

The collection now includes major works by the dean of abstract expressionism, Robert Motherwell; pop masters Roy Lichtenstein, Claes Oldenburg and Jim Dine; the protean Lucas Samaras; minimalists Carl Andre and Agnes Martin; and photo-realist sculptor and Denver native John De Andrea. The photography presentation embraces the medium's short history in depth, from expansive views by William Henry Jackson, whose studio once stood only a few blocks from the DAM's Civic Center site, to contemporary expressions by Coloradoans Robert Adams, Vidie Lange, James Milmoe and Ronald Wohlauer. A section is dedicated to the experimental visions of Sandy Skoglund, Adrian Piper and Gilbert and George. In addition to its burgeoning permanent collection, DAM presents both self-organized and touring temporary exhibitions.

Robert Adams. An annual art show sponsored by the Rotary Club showcases a host of renowned representational painters and sculptors whose works are eagerly sought after.

The Denver Art Museum, the largest general art museum between St. Louis and the West Coast, began life in 1893 as a club formed by cultural grande dame Anne Evans and her circle of art-loving friends. However, the growing collections—including world-class holdings in American Indian art and artifacts—were shunted among Capitol Hill mansions and the nooks and crannies of public buildings until the 1950s. In 1971 Director Otto Karl Bach shepherded the creation of the DAM's first permanent residence, a seven-story "castle" designed by Gio Ponti on Civic Center Park.

At present the DAM comprises significant holdings in the arts of Asia; paintings and sculpture in the European and American tradition; worldwide native arts, especially of Native Americans; textiles and costumes; the arts of the New World, from pre-Columbian times through the Spanish Colonial period; and modern and contemporary art. A new department, Design and Architecture, includes examples of furniture and functional form ranging from English Colonial silver tea services to up-to-the-moment designs of clocks, fabrics and dinnerware from the United States, Italy and Japan.

Although it is the youngest of Denver's "big three" museums, the Denver Museum of Natural History in City Park, incorporated in 1900, is the largest in the Rocky Mountain region and the fifth largest such museum in the United States. By the mid-1990s, it enjoyed an annual attendance of more than 1.5 million visitors. Along with nearly 100 wildlife habitat, scientific and archaeological displays, the museum now features a "prehistoric journey," complete with dinosaur fossils and more; a planetarium; and an IMAX movie theater

TOP: James Rosenquist Exhibition, 1985.

LEFT: The Denver Art Museum, built in 1971, is the work of architects Gio Ponti and James Sudler.

ABOVE: The Arvada Center.

with a four-story screen. It presents a wide variety of temporary exhibitions of art and cultural artifacts from the blockbuster *Ramses II* and *Aztec* shows to more modest, topical exhibits such as master photographer Ansel Adams' spectacular views of the Yosemite Valley.

But not all the glories of Denver's public collections reside in the major museums. Specialized collections and programs abound in smaller public and private centers throughout the metro area. Many are in historic buildings converted to museum use, such as the Foothills Art Center in Golden, once the town's First Presbyterian Church. Now it plays host to the annual Rocky Mountain National Watermedia Exhibition and a full schedule of local and regional shows. In downtown Denver, across the street from the Brown Palace Hotel, stands the stately old Navarre building, a famous—and expensive— brothel during Denver's Silver Boom era. Today it has a more sedate incarnation as the Museum of Western Art, showing masterpieces of frontier American paintings and sculpture: works by George Catlin, Albert Bierstadt and Frederic Remington, even an abstraction by Wyoming-born Jackson Pollock.

TOP: The Navarre building houses the Museum of Western Art.

BOTTOM: The Children's Museum of Denver

In a California Street house that was once the home of well-known black physician Dr. Justina Ford, the Black American West Museum celebrates the history and contributions of African-Americans, from buffalo soldiers and cowboys of the Old West to modern newspaper editors, businesspeople, doctors, teachers and artists.

The Mizel Museum of Judaica on the city's southeast side holds exhibitions that present Colorado's Jewish heritage through works of art, interpreting the shared American experience of immigration and the Jewish component of Colorado's complex ethnic and religious ties.

Denver's newest museum, Museo de las Americas, opened in 1994 in a large renovated storefront in the vibrant Hispanic neighborhood fringing Santa Fe Drive. It is devoted to the traditional and contemporary arts of Latin America and the Caribbean. In its short history, it has already presented national traveling exhibitions and one-artist shows by Latin artists. Museo's director, José Aguayo, articulates the perspective of Denver's entire museum community when he says, "We need to understand and appreciate all these different cultures." Indeed, the area's many museums, large and small, regularly cooperate in the fashion of the legendary West with loans of works and shared projects and programs.

Many regional centers such as the Boulder Museum of Contemporary Art and its new neighbor, the collaborative arts facility known as The Dairy (for the old creamery that provides its home), inhabit reclaimed buildings. Others, including the enchanting Children's Museum of Denver with its look-at-me primary-colored pyramid roof and the splendidly situated Arvada Center for the Arts and Humanities north of Denver, advertise their offerings with dramatic contemporary structures. Arvada underscored its commitment to challenging artwork inside and out with two avant-garde public projects incorporated in its 1992 expansion: Montanan Clarice Dreyer's "Skyline" on the exterior of the Center's amphitheater and, spiraling through the entryway, "Dirt Wall" by internationally known artist Vito Acconci.

Once Denver's museums offered comforting icons of culture to displaced newcomers from distant population centers. Now arts and cultural institutions dot the metro area; the proliferation of new museums reflects the Front Range's inherent diversity and advertises its refinements to visitors from near and far.

84

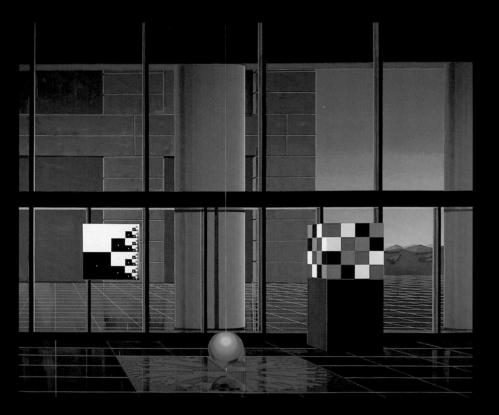

ABOVE: "CORRIDOR #2" BY LUCAS SAMARAS
LEFT: "NUMBER LORE" (DETAIL) BY CLARK RICHERT
BOTTOM: PHOTO OF MARTHA GRAHAM BY BARBARA MORGAN
PHOTOS COURTESY OF THE DENVER ART MUSEUM

"ATHEO SIDE CHAIR" 1993
COURTESY OF THE
DENVER ART MUSEUM

TOP: "THE BROOKLYN BRIDGE"
BY RED GROOMS
UPPER RIGHT: "HARLEQUINS"
BY HARRY MARINSKY
FAR RIGHT: "WINDSONG III"
BY ROBERT MANGOLD
RIGHT: "THE FENCE"
BY CAROLYN BRAAKSMA AND
ANDREW DUFFORD

"Saint Francis of Assisi" by Harry Marinsky
photos courtesy of the Museum of Outdoor Art

"OBEAH 1987" BY ALBERT CHONG

photography

Picture the Denver Area
by Jennifer Heath

*Light is the animating force in photography.
There is a high-voltage quality to a clear
day in Colorado that can burn you out.*
—Robert Adams

In 1853 Solomon Carvalho, with an expedition led by John Charles Fremont, became the first photographer to enter Colorado. Technical limitations meant photography could not yet adequately reflect—as did the dazzling landscape paintings of exploring Europeans—the blazing Western light that has so deeply inspired generations of later photographers. In his memoirs, Carvalho describes a harrowing, wondrous adventure, a journey so arduous it nearly cost him his life, hauling the heavy, awkward equipment he required to make his daguerreotypes. In 1881 his hard work, the precious documentation of a still-pristine wilderness, was lost to fire. One Carvahlo daguerreotype remains and is safely housed in the Library of Congress.

"DYING TULIPS" BY MARK SINK
10"x10" PLATINUM

In *Colorado on Glass: Colorado's First Half Century as Seen Through the Camera* (1975), historian Terry William Mangan recounts that the Rocky Mountains were at first merely an obstacle to the California Gold Rush. But in 1858, when gold was discovered along Cherry Creek, thousands flocked to the area—among them James Sabine, who knew it would be "easier to extract

tures of daunting, behemoth mountains, otherworldly land formations, indefatigable pioneers and exotic inhabitants. Native Americans, ragged and defeated, were exploited with sometimes falsified, frequently dolled-up and romanticized images. The work of photographer Drex Brooks responds to that heady and often brutal era with contemporary photos of Indian battle sites.

TOP: A series of silkscreens by Paula Crane. L TO R: "Requiem #1: Backwater"; "Requiem #2: Castles"; "Requiem #3: Endangered Species"; "Requiem #4: Oversized Load"; "Requiem #5: Clean Sweep." ABOVE: "Mandilon Zapata" from Daniel Salazar's *Macho Sensitivo* series. RIGHT: "Men and Madonna" (Detail) by Gary Emrich, photo emulsion/paper.

gold from the miners' pockets than out of the ground," and so he opened the first Colorado photo studio. He made tintypes, ambrotypes and lantern slides—many tough and touching portraits of men who had left home to seek their fortunes.

The enterprising William Chamberlain left a vast record of life in Colorado in the 1870s. Settlements burgeoned as the railroad burst across the land. By the 1890s, postcards could be mass-produced to titillate stay-at-homes back East with pic-

In 1869 William Henry Jackson began traversing the West as a photographer for the U.S. Geological Survey. He invented or made inventive use of various cameras and developing methods. "Jackson lived through practically every phase of photography from its inception to the 35-millimeter camera," says Christopher James, whose marvelous contemporary photographs include startling night landscapes and a series created in 1994 that echoes Jackson's

Denver panoramas, a sort of before-and-after, using identical perspectives. "Buildings in Jackson's landscape of Capitol Hill [a Denver-area landmark] show up in mine," James says, "but in a totally new and different surrounding."

In 1879 Jackson purchased Chamberlain's lucrative photo gallery on Denver's Larimer Street. His last studio is now the site of the

Women's Bank in Denver. By the time he died, Jackson was established as Colorado's most renowned and respected photographer.

Today that honor belongs to Robert Adams, a recipient of the prestigious MacArthur Fellowship, otherwise known as the "genius award." Adams' photographs give tender, handsome form to the ugliness that so-called "progress" has imposed on the Western landscape. Through the ferocious loveliness captured by his lens, he makes us aware, without polemic, of ecological misuse and abuse. These are stark, poetic, black and white compositions, full of commonplace beauty.

Land and place are of particular concern as well to photographers such as Ken Abbott and Eric Paddock, curator of photography at the Colorado Historical Society. Abbott creates sad, loving, compassionate pictures profoundly striking for their ordinariness: neighborhoods and trailer parks, farmhouses and peaceful rural areas in the process of demolition by encroaching development. The Denver metro area's incredible growth rate, the changes and the nostalgia they engender, have become a theme, mirroring the underside of urban expansion.

James Balog expresses environmental suffering with slick, anthropomorphized portraits of zoo animals and endangered species that resemble

fashion photography—requiems to the dignity of once free and wild creatures documented in three highly praised books.

Of course, environmental photography does not necessarily imply a natural setting. "Place" is often depicted by Latino photographers through culture and communities that endure despite poverty, oppression and racism. Exquisite works by artists such as Judy Miranda and Virginia Garcia not only celebrate Hispanic peoples and life but enlighten, empower and give fresh insight into the

"Eagle River at Avon"
by Kent Gunnufson

richness of diversity. Daniel Salazar's series *Macho Sensitivo* explores Chicano male identity through hilarious photo-constructions employing figures from the Mexican Revolution's pre-eminent photographer, Augustin Victor Casasola, and juxtaposing them with stereotypical "female" trappings and icons to re-evaluate hackneyed notions of *machismo*. Thus, a military junta sports scarlet tutus and Geronimo struggles with overflowing grocery bags.

Albert Chong's powerful, mythic photographs are also discourses with ancestors—rituals that evoke magic and spirit and describe a personal mysticism born of his Asian and African heritage. Gary Sweeney's witty and ironic "America, Why I Love Her"—a part of the Collection of the City and County of Denver and on permanent display at Denver International Airport—makes irreverent, affectionate fun of the Euro-cultural landscape.

Located at DIA's domestic baggage claim area, the piece illustrates the artist's travels throughout the United States via a map of the country's most eccentric roadside attractions like California's Barbie Doll Hall of Fame and the Boll Weevil Monument in Alabama.

The Denver Salon is a group of photographers who have joined together to show their work and exchange ideas in photo experimentation. The Salon held the first Internet art exhibition, *Off the Highway*, engineered by Denver's Rule Gallery and photographer Mark Sink, whose ethereal work includes manipulated Polaroid photographs and fuzzy, romantic images created with a toy camera called the Diana.

A part of the Collection of the City and County of Denver, Barbara Jo Revelle's "Colorado Panorama: A People's History" spans two city blocks along the Denver Convention Center. A far cry from tintypes and wetplates, the mural is computer-digitalized and built with small tiles to offer a view of regional history through the faces of its people, many of them often overlooked by traditional canons of society.

In 1860 the *Rocky Mountain Herald* made approving reference to a "Miss Mickel," photographer and proprietor of the Ladies Ambrotype Gallery. Three months after its grand opening, Miss Mickel's studio closed. According to Mangan, there were a surprising number of women photographers in the early days, but few are remembered. It was not until the 1930s, when Denver native Laura Gilpin—author of *The Enduring Navajo*—garnered national

RIGHT: **"Montana Sankai" by Caroline Hinkley, computer-generated cactus print, lead inkjet-silverprint.**
BELOW: **"Departure" by Christopher James.**

acclaim that women's photographic achievements were seriously recognized.

Some of Colorado's prominent contemporary female photographers include Jennifer O'Meara, whose inkjet digital print "Play Hard" is a part of the Collection of the City and County of Denver and on permanent display at McNichols Sports Arena; Caroline Hinkley, whose deconstructionist assemblages are strong, supercharged sociopolitical indictments; Kay Obering, whose extraordinary, sweeping vision encompasses the Botanic Gardens—shaped into a majestic, participatory photo installation—as well as works that chronicle the politics of reproductive rights; Valari Jack, a portraitist whose comtemplative gaze has rested on the daily lives of the Sisters of St. Walburga at their abbey outside Boulder; and

tional work, art photos and photo-documentary. One exhibition combined a 1948 *Life* magazine photo essay, *The Country Doctor* by W. Eugene Smith shot in Kremmling, Colorado, with *Portrait of a City Hospital,* the poignant, evocative contemporary reportage of Bernard Mendoza, taken at Denver General Hospital. That series, a part of the Collection of the City and County of Denver, is on display at the hospital.

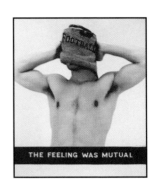

THE FEELING WAS MUTUAL

The world of photography has evolved in leaps and bounds since the days of daguerrotypes and lantern slides. "In a sense," Virginia Garcia says, "photography—the silver-gelatin process—is a dying art."

"There is an incredibly rich array of ways in which a photograph can be made," writes photographer John Bonath. "The commonly known

ABOVE: **"The Feeling Was Mutual" by Jack Balas.** LEFT: **Untitled by Barbara Jo Revelle**

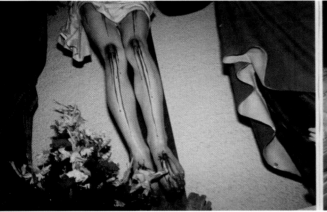

Melanie Walker, whose gorgeous, handmade "staged" pieces fabricate a life's story through fictionalized memory.

Miss Mickel's misfortunes notwithstanding, Camera Obscura, owned by photographer Hal Gould, has long been central to the Denver area's photographic needs. The intimate Bannock Street gallery, across from the Denver Art Museum, is fondly referred to by photographers as "the source." It provides photographers and the public with national and international exhibitions of contemporary and vintage photos from Cartier to Ansel Adams to postmodernist Les Krims.

The Grant Gallery on Market Street has been cited as one of the best photo venues in the country. Owner John Grant's repertoire is various and fascinating, balancing experimental and tradi-

processes are only the tip of an iceberg of possibilities. Electrical and magnetic developments evolve daily in the area of digital cameras and the realm of the computer. This is truly a medium constantly redefining itself."

Denver-area artist R. Edward Lowe is a pioneer in holographic imagery and has received widespread recognition for his innovations. His work is in the permanent collection of the Denver Art Museum. Gary Emrich has created astonishing photographic installations at Denver's Robischon Gallery using liquid light. These definitions and applications of photography would have been unthinkable to Carvalho, Jackson or Miss Mickel.

The future of photography is unimaginable, even to us.

THREE PHOTOS FROM *PORTRAIT OF A CITY HOSPITAL* BY BERNARD MENDOZA, PART OF THE COLLECTION OF THE CITY AND COUNTY OF DENVER

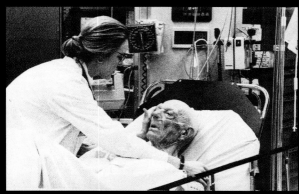

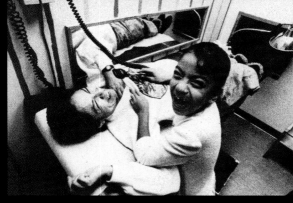

TOP: "TRAPPER GEORGE,
BRECKENRIDGE" BY KENT GUNNUFSON
ABOVE: "SOUTH OF NEW RAYMER, CO"
BY DAVID SHARPE
RIGHT: "GERONIMO CON GROCERIES"
FROM *MACHO SENSITIVO*
BY DANIEL SALAZAR

LEFT: "UFO CITYSCAPE"
BY ERIC HELLAND
TOP: "FIRST THANATOGRAPHIC WORK"
1981 BY ERIC HAVELOCK-BAILIE
MIDDLE: "THE OLD MAN AND THE APE"
© 1995 JAMES BALOG. FROM JAMES
BALOG'S BOOK *ANIMA*, PUBLISHED BY
ARTS ALTERNATIVE PRESS,
BOULDER, CO.
BOTTOM: "CAMOUFLAGE"
BY MELANIE WALKER

101

ABOVE: UNTITLED PHOTO FROM
THE SERIES *MODELS, ACTORS
AND OTHER REMARKABLE
CITIZENS* BY PAUL SCHRODER
RIGHT: "LISA" BY MARK SINK

ABOVE: PHOTO BY VIRGINIA GARCIA

LEFT: "AT VESPERS" FROM THE DOCUMENTARY
*QUIET SEASONS OF GRACE: A YEAR IN THE LIFE OF
THE ABBEY OF ST. WALBURGA* BY VALARI JACK

TOP: "BOTANIC GARDENS"(DETAIL) BY KAY OBERING

LEFT: "ABANDONED FARMHOUSE, MARSHALL, CO, MAY 1995" © KEN ABBOTT

"Ferris Wheel"
© 1994 Christopher James

performing arts

The Stage Alive!
by M.S. Mason

Rarely does a contemporary theater production meet with the wild national acclaim of *Black Elk Speaks*. Yet this ambitious play, brought from the book to the stage by the Denver Center Theatre Company's Donovan Marley for the 1993-1994 season, sold out nightly wherever it toured. Every curtain brought a standing ovation for the Native American cast, and critics from New York to Los Angeles lauded the leading-edge work as a poetic and mythic history offering a healing vision for human brotherhood.

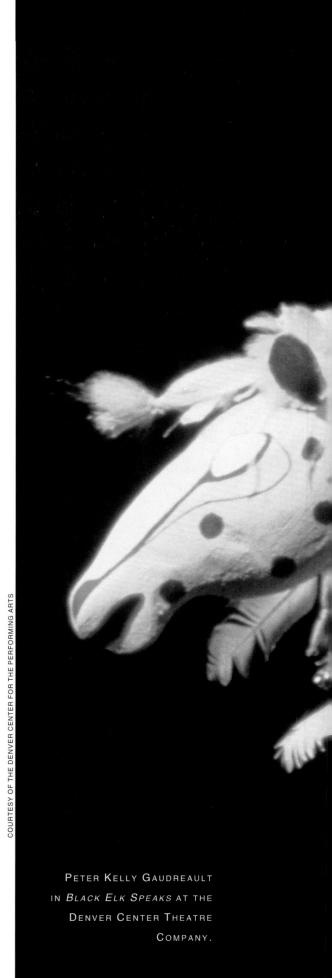

COURTESY OF THE DENVER CENTER FOR THE PERFORMING ARTS

PETER KELLY GAUDREAULT
IN *BLACK ELK SPEAKS* AT THE
DENVER CENTER THEATRE
COMPANY.

In this age of Hollywood technological marvels, it is unusual for a play to take off so suddenly and vibrantly. But Denver audiences are accustomed to the magic of the stage. The love affair is evidenced by the number and variety of theaters that have sprouted over the past 20 years. Year by year, talent flows into the area to join the existing pool. The "immigrant" actors, designers, directors and playwrights are not only seeking a quality of life found nowhere else in the country but are answering the call of a burgeoning and increasingly important scene.

The Denver Center Theatre Company, a division of the Denver Center for the Performing Arts, is the region's largest and most prestigious. It presents polished, highly professional productions, many of them risk-taking and experimental. Conventional wisdom suggests that audiences prefer the tried and true. Certainly, the DCTC satisfies with a fair share of solid classics and popular modern plays, but, as Gully Stanford of the Denver Center for the Performing Arts notes, increased experimentation infuses the entire theater-going experience with new life. The people are coming.

It is the nature of theater that neither the eye nor the mind can be led. In a live production, there can be no passivity. Many of today's plays are meant to question assumptions and debunk prejudice. Viewers are challenged to confront their own ideas about the "way things are."

The DCTC's *Star Fever* is a case in point. Czech playwright/designer/director Pavel M. Dobrusky created a highly controversial look at Western civilization in the 1990s. Based very loosely on *The Baccae* by Euripides, the complex tragicomedy exposed the nature of contemporary idolatry—the worship of celebrities—and the resulting spiritual vacuum. The play's form is raw, abrasive and defiant, and its message that television degrades the human spirit and therefore transmits the raging "star fever" provoked vigorous debate and launched the center's 1994-1995 season with a bang.

TOP: **Stuart Bird, John Belindo and Peter Kelly Gaudreault in *Black Elk Speaks*.**
COURTESY OF THE DENVER CENTER FOR THE PERFORMING ARTS

BOTTOM: **The Temple Hoyne Buell Theatre at the Denver Performing Arts Complex**
COURTESY DENVER METRO CONVENTION & VISITORS BUREAU

RIGHT: *Black Elk Speaks*
PHOTO BY TERRY SHAPIRO

Post-performance discussions, for *Star Fever* and *Black Elk Speaks* as well as for other pieces, are invigorating; audiences become profoundly involved. The "talk-backs" provide a place for questions; expressions of confusion, concern or appreciation; and a means by which people can come to terms with a play's wrenching issues. In turn, they help stimulate the entire theater scene.

Smaller companies also attract amazing talent and produce splendid work. Germinal Stage Denver, CityStage Ensemble, Eulipions, Hunger Artists, Industrial Arts Theatre, Compass Theatre, the Mirror Players, Theatre on Broadway, the Avenue Theatre, the Arvada Center for the Arts and Humanities, the Aurora Fox Arts Center, The Changing Scene, Denver Civic Theatre, El Centro Su Teatro, Theater in the Park and PHAMALy, along with many excellent community and children's theater groups, are incredibly diverse in style and mission.

L ee Massaro moved to Denver from New York City because she and her husband, actor Erik Tieze, wanted a dog, a house and a baby. They also wanted to work "all the time." For Massaro, artistic director of Industrial Arts Theatre, it's about putting humanity on stage. Industrial Arts grapples with various subject matter, most reflecting socially responsible themes. The work is consistently born out of human impulses, heartfelt and beautifully acted, designed and directed.

And so, too, are the shows produced by Eulipions, one of the area's greatest treasures. The small company of African-American actors and singers has created memorable productions of old and new plays by African-American playwrights. *Ain't Misbehaving*, *Shakin' the Mess Outta Misery* and *Black Nativity* brought with them serious insights into the culture's life and thought. The warmth and intelligence of such works are profoundly and universally inspiring.

El Centro Su Teatro, headed and co-founded by award-winning playwright Tony Garcia, stages plays by such Mexican-American luminaries as Luis Valdez (perhaps best known for *Zoot Suit*) as well as original pieces such as Garcia's magnificent *La Carpa Aztlan Presents: I Don't Speak English Only*, which refers to politi-

cal issues employing the Mexican tent-vaudeville style of the '20s and '30s. Like Eulipions', Su Teatro's presentations not only function as art but as paths leading toward cultural empathy and empowerment. Both groups also provide ongoing participatory activities and marvelous programs for youngsters.

CityStage Ensemble's mission is likewise socially conscious. Longtime member Terry Burnsed describes the work of CSE as "reflecting a greater consciousness between stylistic adventurousness and the social and political implications of the text." The company does the classics right along with tough modern plays, but every refinement adds a bite. Audiences never leave a CSE production without something to think about.

Ed Baierlein, artistic director for Germinal Stage Denver, says his company is less adventurous now than when it started in the 1960s, because audiences have changed. Nevertheless, Germinal continues to take on difficult plays and rise to the demands they present. The outstanding work is consistently cerebral and entertaining.

The rise of Theatre on Broadway is another of Denver's many success stories. In the capable hands of artistic director Steve Tangedal, TOB's work grows steadily stronger with marvelous productions like *Six Degrees of Separation* and exceptional actors such as Deborah Persoff.

"I love working with such dedicated people, and I love helping to bring a great experience to the audience," says TOB Managing Director Tim Albo. "The demand for theater [alternatives] has increased. The thrill of live theater cannot be duplicated. No two performances are the same. Part of that thrill is social, too. You're all experiencing it together."

Alternative theater notwithstanding, the classics will always be in demand. Denver is home to two wonderful companies working in language-based and traditional theater. Shakespeare's plays have received stunning, inventive treatment from both the Ad Hoc Theatre's James Gale and Compass Theatre's Christopher Selbie,

PHOTO BY ALEX HABENICHT

PHOTO BY ALEX HABENICHT

COURTESY DENVER METRO CONVENTION & VISITORS BUREAU

TOP: **The Temple Hoyne Buell Theatre opened at the Denver Performing Arts Complex in 1991. The 9,200-seat complex is the second largest in the country; only Lincoln Center is bigger.**
LEFT, TOP AND BOTTOM:
Oklahoma!
by Englewood Summer Drama

yet the two directors exercise radically different styles. These contrasts and juxtapositions of imagination immeasurably enrich the theater and its patrons.

The Avenue Theatre has gained a well-deserved reputation for the best in comedy. Artistic Director John Ashton frequently opts for off-beat delights like *The Search for Intelligent*

Life in the Universe and *Later Life*. Sometimes, he chooses highly accessible shows, but even *The Odd Couple* had a twist in the Avenue's production; the two beloved curmudgeon bachelor roommates were transformed into women, making the hilarity all the more pointed.

At The Changing Scene—one of Denver's oldest experimental venues—the plays are inevitably risky, premiere productions, many by local playwrights. "Here the whole thing is an act of love," says owner Al Brooks. "Our [affiliated] dance studio has sustained us, but the plays are done by directors who feel they must do them." This creative imperative ranges wildly in style and artistic merit, and no city would be complete without places like The Changing Scene, willing to take enormous chances to foster emerging concepts.

In Boulder the Colorado Dance Festival often veers from the expected into the unfamiliar realms of "new performance," venturing beyond dance and even dance-theater. Across the years, the CDF has imported plays by John Jesrun and performance art by internationally renowned artists such as Guillermo Gomez-Peña, Rachel Rosenthal, George Emilio Sanchez and Kip Fulbeck, among other surprising and felicitous productions.

The Bug Performance and Media Arts Center provides both a space and a kind of laboratory for new performance that is mostly area-generated. The Bug brings to light the work of exciting young actors, artists, musicians, filmmakers and videographers. It was co-founded by Hugh Graham, who—with David Walker and Ray Schelgunov—ad-libs an ongoing series of "lectures and dialogues" called *Home Medical Shopping Network*, witty and caustic commentary on contemporary American life.

One need not look far for proof of the breadth and depth of theater in Denver. Banding together, physically handicapped amateur actors—aptly calling themselves PHAMALy—are dedicated to fine musicals. In Littleton the South Suburban Theatre

Company and the Main Street Players represent the very best in community theater, as do the Boulder Repertory and Boulder Actors Ensemble. At the Naropa Institute, theater is taught by veterans of New York's Living Theatre, while the Victorian team of Gilbert & Sullivan is immortalized with seasonal productions of their madcap operettas at the University of Colorado.

Meanwhile, mainstream theaters such as the Arvada Center for the Arts and Humanities and the Aurora Fox Arts Center not only stage professional, popular theater but also many children's plays. The Arvada Center offers several standing-room-only children's theater productions each season. Among the triumphs is a charming, revisionist fairytale, *What Really Happened Once Upon A Time*, by Denver playwright Pamela Clifton.

Henry Lowenstein is considered the "father" of theater in Denver. His loving and meticulous nurturing brought the Denver Center for the Performing Arts to life, and his tireless efforts and unerring, generous support can be credited for the power and dynamism of the scene today. His Denver Civic Theatre is ever-pioneering, cultivating new work as well as producing established pieces and consistently lending its space to various companies from Compass to the fledgingly annual Latino Dance Festival.

Actor and audience have a reciprocal relationship. Nothing can replace the human touch, especially in this electronic age. The very limitations of the stage are part of its glory, for the viewer's imagination is not tied to image nor to words alone but to the actors' interpretation of word and image. The actors tell our stories, and reflect our concerns, joys, fears, hopes, strengths and weaknesses. They are as large as life, but no larger, and so the experience they offer us in the theater is unique and satisfying.

THE COLORADO SHAKESPEARE FESTIVAL
M.S. Mason

In 1992 *Time* magazine named the Colorado Shakespeare Festival at the University of Colorado in Boulder one of the country's top three.

It was a well-deserved accolade for a marvelous summer event that has taken place for nearly four decades to honor the Bard. Outdoors under the stars in the Mary Rippon Theatre, actors enlighten and entertain 42,000 audience members each season with glorious, imaginative and varying productions. The full moon gleams over a gorgeous and elaborate, heart-wrenching staging of *King Lear*, a stark "Generation X" presentation of *Hamlet* or an amusing *As You Like It* in fin de siecle dress. Comfortably ensconced on pillows that soften the stone amphitheater seats or hunkering down in the grass, visitors and Coloradans revel in the explosive power of *Julius Caesar* and the whimsy of *A Midsummer Night's Dream*, the terror of *MacBeth* and the sexual politics of *The Taming of The Shrew*.

CSF actors are students, semi-professionals and professionals, some of whom—Val Kilmer, Michael Moriarty, Annette Bening, Joe Spano and Charles Siebert—have gone on to fame. Long before television's *L.A. Law*, Jimmy Smits trod the CSF boards as a confused, ferocious-but-tender Othello.

Fine costumes, fantastic lighting and dazzling set design are all part of the magic. But the CSF's most important contribution to the art of theater may lie in its lessons. The best training any young actor can receive comes with the opportunity to perform the dynamic roles Shakespeare created.

DEBORAH PERSOFF AND STEVEN
TANGEDAHL IN *LAUGHING WILD* AT THEATRE
ON BROADWAY. PHOTO COURTESY OF
THEATRE ON BROADWAY

ACTORS ENSEMBLE
PERFORMS *ELEEMOSYNARY*
AT THE GUILD THEATRE
IN BOULDER.
PHOTO BY ED GREENBERG

ROXANNE BROWN AS
BILLIE HOLIDAY IN EULIPIONS' *LADY
DAY AT EMERSON'S BAR & GRILL.*
PHOTO BY PAUL SCHRODER

KEITH HATTEN, PHILLIP GASKIN AND
ROBERT EVANS IN *THE COLORED
MUSEUM* BY EULIPIONS.
PHOTO BY PAUL SCHRODER

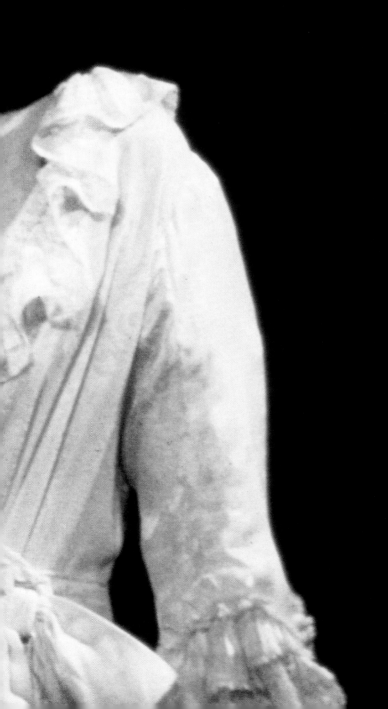

THE PHANTOM OF THE OPERA,
PRESENTED BY ROBERT GARNER
CENTER ATTRACTIONS, THE TOURING
BROADWAY SHOW DIVISION OF THE
DENVER CENTER FOR THE PERFORMING
ARTS.
COURTESY OF THE DENVER CENTER FOR
THE PERFORMING ARTS

The Body Moves
by Jennifer Heath

There are no sufficient words to describe how dance lifts us into that expanse which mingles with the infinite. The Colorado Ballet, the David Taylor Dance Theatre and Cleo Parker Robinson Dance Ensemble have for decades provided Colorado with beauty and rhapsodic, lush artistry that offer joy and stimulus to the spirit. With the Colorado Dance Festival, the Naropa Institute and the University of Colorado's Theatre and Dance Department on center stage as prime purveyors of New Dance, the region has experienced a "talent rush" of innovative, provocative and highly individual post-postmodern performers redefining the range of gesture and expression we usually consider "dance."

CARMELA WEBER,
VERTICAL DANCE
PHOTO BY CAROLE CARDON

LEFT: KEITH TERRY
PHOTO BY RICK DER
COURTESY OF THE COLORADO
DANCE FESTIVAL

"I think of new dance as a hybrid of forms," says CDF Associate Artistic Director Judith Hussie. "It's based in a modern-dance tradition, yet the artist might work with a pastiche of, say, hip-hop, gymnastics, martial arts and modern dance." Each summer the Festival becomes a cornucopia of inspiration that nourishes area artists with an array of teachers and performers from every conceivable world view and aesthetic point of view. Ralph Lemon, Eiko and Koma, Dana Reitz, GhettOriginal hip-hop dancers, Trisha Brown, Urban Bush Women, Mel Wong, Sin Cha Hong, Molissa Fenley, Bill T. Jones, Merian Soto—the list is endless and endlessly diverse. The Festival constantly pushes dance boundaries, illustrating that creativity has no borders, no fixed patterns, no one soul. With every artist, dance is reconfigured.

Barbara Dilley at the Naropa Institute is a former Merce Cunningham dancer, veteran of the vital Judson Dance Theatre and explosive Grand Union of the 1960s and early '70s, and a renowned choreographer in her own right. Based on years of Buddhist meditation combined with modern American improvisational techniques, she is evolving techniques of stillness and awareness in dance. Her soft, sensual phrasings and the contemplative musicality in her movements are exquisite.

Dilley designed the Institute's 20-year-old Dance/Movement Studies Department and imports teachers such as Kei Takei or Judson alumni Steve Paxton, Simone Forti and Yvonne Rainer. In tandem with dancer Diane Butler, director of the Institute's InterArts Studies program, Dilley has built a home for experimentation and a safe haven in which to investigate interdisciplinary collaborations.

Any given performance might find Butler tumbling about the stage weaving Paxton's Con-

PHOTO BY MARY GEARHART
COURTESY OF THE COLORADO
DANCE FESTIVAL

PHOTO BY RICHARD PETERSON

PHOTO BY DeCROCE

**UPPER LEFT: Sarah Skaggs
ABOVE: Stacy Smith and Peter Davison in
Lynne Taylor-Corbett's "Appearances" at the David
Taylor Dance Theatre. LEFT: Kim Robards choreographed
"Sentient Fury" for herself and Ronnie Whittaker.
RIGHT: *Swan Lake***

tact Improvisation with balletic techniques or applying adventurous modern-dance styles to Balinese gamelan music. She and Dilley—along with Carol McDowell and Polly Motley, who together form the Mariposa Collective—invite students and audiences to understand that rigid end-results are not the point, that art is found within the process.

Motley is a rising star on the national new dance scene, garnering rave reviews from major critics. *Village Voice* critic Deborah Jowitt calls Motley's body "a map whose contours and attitudes graph a cultural and personal profile." Her fluidity and happy eagerness give an impression of sheer spontaneity and utter arbitrariness, which belie the careful structure mooring the work.

The black-box Charlotte York Irey Theatre on the CU campus is one of the area's finest venues. In the 1940s Irey pulled the CU dance program away

from the Physical Education Department, then shaped, guided and developed it for many years. Today the Dance Department is directed by Nada Diachenko, formerly of the Erick Hawkins Dance Company, a bright force who has further opened dance definitions for an upcoming generation.

Out of CU's fecund ground have come such marvels as Kim Robards, whose dance company

CLEO PARKER ROBINSON
A HEALING DANCE

Jennifer Heath

Twenty-five years ago a young Denver native with limited resources beyond her own visions and huge talent founded a modern-dance ensemble. She was inspired by many mentors, especially Rita Berger, a former George Balanchine dancer, and the legendary dancer/ethnologist Katherine Dunham. She studied with Merce Cunningham, the Alvin Ailey American Dance Centre and the Dance Theatre of Harlem.

But among Cleo Parker Robinson's deepest influences were segregation, bigotry and prejudice.

At a time when there were few African-American dance companies and even fewer opportunities for black dancers, Robinson recruited kids from the ghettos, streets and schoolyards to create what was to become one of the finest and most energetic organizations in the country. She has changed people's lives, metamorphosed the grim present into brilliant futures. Her school is a training center for her professional ensemble as well as a place for others simply to express themselves through dance. In addition she recently launched Project Self-Discovery, a national program for at-risk youth.

And there is so much more. The company has toured internationally; Robinson has taught workshops from Belize to Iceland; she has received choreography fellowships and commissions; collaborated with world-class poets, filmmakers and composers; and even assisted in the formation of the National Dance Company of the Bahamas. Tributes, honors and awards have poured in from every corner of the globe.

"My father warned me, 'You were born with three strikes against you: you're a woman, an artist and half white,' " Robinson once told an interviewer. Crosses were burned in front of the family's Denver home; the little girl, who was teaching dance at the University of Colorado by the age of 15, was witness to unspeakable racism.

Yet Robinson's is a story of absolute triumph, a testimony to her unflagging belief that dance is a universal and healing language.

is growing, as it were, in leaps and bounds. Robards' are not fancy, big-budget productions; nevertheless, they've lately been stealing the spotlight and gaining wide recognition. A minimalist choreographer, Robards sketches clear, tight, energetic pieces that make profound use of the body's visceral power.

Body and place are very much at play in the

MARDA KIRN
A NEW PATH

Jennifer Heath

Marda Kirn landed in Boulder about two decades ago fresh from Sarah Lawrence. She taught ballet and scheduled classes at the Community Free School. Soon, dance was the school's largest offering. So why stop there?

Kirn produced the Boulder Dance Festival through the city's ArtsFest. It was successful, so what could be more natural than to build an internationally renowned festival? Anyone would, of course.

David White, director of Manhattan's famous Dance Theater Workshop, enjoys relating how Kirn manifested her dream singlehandedly "out of the back of her blue Volkswagen bug," stuffed with files, photos, grant applications and a sleeping bag. Thirteen years later, the Colorado Dance Festival is one of the most important summer dance celebrations in the United States.

As artistic director, her vision is impeccable. Kirn brings not only the best-known contemporary performers, but she seeks constantly to locate and present worldwide traditional dance. And she has a fearless, uncanny knack for knowing and producing cutting-edge performers. Across the years she has not only enriched audiences throughout the area, she has encouraged the growth of the dance community in all its diverse forms and her leadership has helped bring national attention to many local groups. In 1990 she received a Colorado Governor's Award for Excellence in the Arts.

At Sarah Lawrence, Kirn recalls, mythographer Joseph Campbell once told her, "When you follow a path, it means someone has been there before. Make your own path." She has never ceased heeding her teacher's advice.

choreography of Carmela Weber and Nancy Smith Hall. Weber makes rigorous "vertical dances": she climbs walls and dances there. It is an art—not sport—through which she says she is "attempting to create a new vocabulary." Smith Hall also yanks dance off the ground with Frequent Flyers, a low-flying trapeze/aerial dance ensemble, whose work is often site-spe-

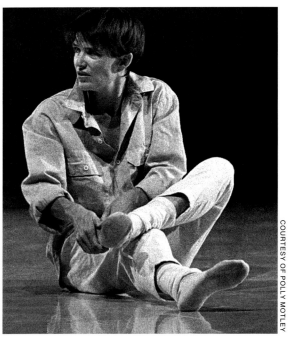

COURTESY OF POLLY MOTLEY

Polly Motley of the Mariposa Collective.

cific, taking place at drive-in theaters, on proscenium stages, in parks and in churches.

Perhaps the high, breathless mountains and the dizzying spaciousness of the plains inspire these artists and others, like Peter Davison, to suspend their dances between earth and sky. Davison—a member of the much-loved juggling/movement trio Airjazz, Colorado Repertory and David Taylor Dance Theatre—is one of the area's most charming, highest soaring dancers. It's as if he were built of sails. No wonder Davison says his boyhood idols were Alexander Calder and Batman.

"Dance is just life out loud!"
—Cleo Parker Robinson

But for the David Taylor Dance Theatre, dance is much larger than life. Since 1979 Taylor has presided over his company as director, inventor, dancer, choreographer and impresario.

His interests in the metaphysical and the mysteries of exotic cultures are at the core of his ritualistic and stylized concerts. Dramatic and lavishly produced, Taylor's presentations employ multimedia effects, unconventional lighting and extravagant sounds, costumes and sets. Area artists, musicians and guest choreographers collaborate with Taylor to create a reper-

COURTESY OF THE ARVADA CENTER FOR ARTS AND HUMANITIES

toire of thought-provoking and entertaining ballet works with strong roots in modern dance.

A dancer for more than two decades, Taylor performed *The Nutcracker* so often, he says, he finally "got very sick of it." His solution, ever adroit, was to reinterpret it. In his hands, the perennially popular Christmas pageant with its Victorian fairytale motifs was transformed into art-deco surrealism.

Whether "deco-fied" or purist, annual productions of *The Nutcracker* sustain and enrich regional ballet companies as well as children's imaginations. The 35-year-old Colorado Ballet's customary version never fails to thrill audiences. Year after year kids of all ages stumble out of the splendid production dazzled and enchanted.

The Ballet naturally offers a rich, compelling lineup of other favorites— *Swan Lake*, *Cinderella*, *Billy the Kid* or *Romeo and Juliet*. Artistic Director Martin Fredmann also extends the company's repertoire into contemporary realms, experimenting, for example, with a suite of his own creation, *A Little Love*, with music by Nina Simone. George Balanchine's choreography was recently gorgeously reconstructed, movement by move-

ment, a challenge for perfection that Fredmann and his dancers met fearlessly and delightfully.

Colorado Ballet is considered among the most disciplined, resilient, intricate and lyrical of regional companies. Fredmann has collected electrifying dancers from around the world. Whatever Fredmann's magic, it is effective. A daring debut in New York met with fine praise

LORENZO RAMIREZ
PRESERVING THE LIFE

Jennifer Heath

When Lorenzo Ramirez was 16, living in Cheyenne, Wyoming, he got his first taste of Mexican folk dance. It changed his life. "The beauty and rhythm hit me like a ton of bricks," he recalls. "I played drums, but I didn't know you could make the same rhythms with your feet. I'd been searching for an identity, to know my history, so I was allowed to move to Denver to attend the Escuela Tlatelolco."

The alternative school at Denver's Crusade for Justice—a Chicano version of New York's School for Performing Arts—provided just the impetus and surprise he needed. "I didn't know I could dance."

He performed with three other groups before he founded El Grupo Folklorico Sabor Latino in 1988, with young dancers currently ranging in age from 14 to 25. At 38 Ramirez is Sabor Latino's oldest member. He finds time to choreograph, teach, direct and administer. "This group, I call my own. The others were dying off, people got married, got tired, were leaving. But I knew these dances had to be passed on. I can't dance forever. I want to make sure it continues at the level it is now."

Ramirez travels throughout Mexico seeking authentic dances with costumes of all regions to add to Sabor Latino's repertoire, which extends far beyond standards and favorites like the Mexican hat dance. "We have also tried to expand into other areas of Latino dance, but the demand is too great for Mexican folklore." The variations in Mexican cultures alone, with Indian, Spanish, Arabic and other influences, make it an endless source of richness and diversity.

Sabor Latino travels all over the American West, and its reputation is growing internationally. An upcoming tour of Mexico will "be the first time we've gone there to perform rather than to learn." A triumph, to say the least.

and brought the Colorado Ballet well-deserved national attention.

Critics, audiences and presenters worldwide welcome the Cleo Parker Robinson Dance Ensemble with shamelessly flattering adjectives: "spirited," "eye-catching," "exuberant," "acute," "celebratory," "superb," "stunning."

Impassioned, joyful athleticism and poignant

L TO R:

Charles "Honi" Coles, Steve Condos, Jimmy Slyde, Eddie Brown and Gregory Hines.

PHOTO BY BILL WARREN

LIVING LEGENDS

Jennifer Heath

Some ideas are ahead of their times. This one was also just in the nick of time.

In 1986 the Colorado Dance Festival developed the first two-week model for presenting rhythm tap dance, with classes and conferences that gathered artists, dance scholars and historians. Jazz-tap greats of the 1930s and '40s appeared in sold-out performances, in jam-packed proscenium theaters and in Denver's historic Casino Cabaret. This jazz nightclub, in its heyday, had regularly presented these "swelle-gant," elegant dancing percussionists, and was reclaimed by the CDF for the event.

Among the all-but-forgotten superstars were Charles "Honi" Coles, Steve Condos, Cholly Atkins, Eddie Brown, Bunny Briggs, LaVaughn Robinson and Jimmy Slyde. Even *The Cotton Club* movie star Gregory Hines showed up to pay tribute and glide around the floor with these men who had been his teachers. The aged performers graced Colorado stages and studios with their showstopping tap fusillades, their light, clear syncopations and their wonderful memories. Coloradans were dazzled.

Similar conferences soon sprang up around the United States and in Europe honoring the pioneer hoofers and featuring a new generation of rhythm tappers, mentored by the old. The CDF spearheaded an International Tap Association that strives to preserve this essential American cultural legacy, to keep the history of tap alive and the art form kicking.

The dance festival's tap reunions continued annually through 1992. The events came none too soon. One by one these legends are fading. Honi Coles, Steve Condos and Eddie Brown all died within two years of each other. The world will never sound the same.

elegance mingle in pieces that pay tribute to Aretha Franklin or Duke Ellington, to gospel or to family, works which often grapple with contemporary African-American experience. Robinson's dancers reflect Katherine Dunham's idiosyncratic mixture of balletic and Afro-Caribbean styles, juxtapositions of cultures, gloriously and narratively executed.

Robinson's special genius has been to commission revered choreographers, such as Dunham, Talley Beatty, Donald McKayle and David Rousseve, to choreograph pieces around her magnificent dancers, thereby stretching their abilities and thrusting the company into a far larger arena. Ultimately, her deep concern for community and the notion of artist-as-cultural-ambassador are the bases on which she builds her amazing ensemble.

Community action and outreach are also motivating factors for Lorenzo Ramirez, who has plucked young Latino dancers out of precarious situations and given them avocation through El Grupo Folklorico Sabor Latino. In the past several years, Sandra Santa Cruz has been revitalizing the community with a Colorado Latino Dance Festival, an invitational exhibition of dance that highlights Latino heritage in all its wonderful, shape-shifting aspects: the stateliness of flamenco; ancient, alchemical Mayan and Aztec dance forms; lively, enlivening Afro-Cuban rhythms.

At Moyo Nguvu Cultural Arts Center, the brilliant urgency of African dance is reclaimed and passed on. At the Denver and Nederland powwows, breathtaking Native American dancers keep tribal traditions alive. Middle Eastern dance thrives. Battalions of ordinary folk put on their dancin' shoes and swirl, whirl, clog and twirl to folk dances and salsa.

"The strongest artists," Judith Hussie notes, "are those with unique voices. The most powerful usually come from artists rooted in artistic and cultural traditions, that relationship between where we've come from and where we're going. Artists who respect tradition but also, as Ezra Pound said, who 'make it new.'"

JAWOLE WILLA JO ZOLLAR OF URBAN BUSH WOMEN
COURTESY OF THE COLORADO DANCE FESTIVAL

TOP: "ANCIENT AIRS," CHOREOGRAPHED BY KIM ROBARDS
PHOTO BY RICHARD PETERSON COURTESY OF KIM ROBARDS DANCE
BOTTOM: "RAINDANCE," CHOREOGRAPHED BY MILTON MYERS
COURTESY OF CLEO PARKER ROBINSON DANCE ENSEMBLE

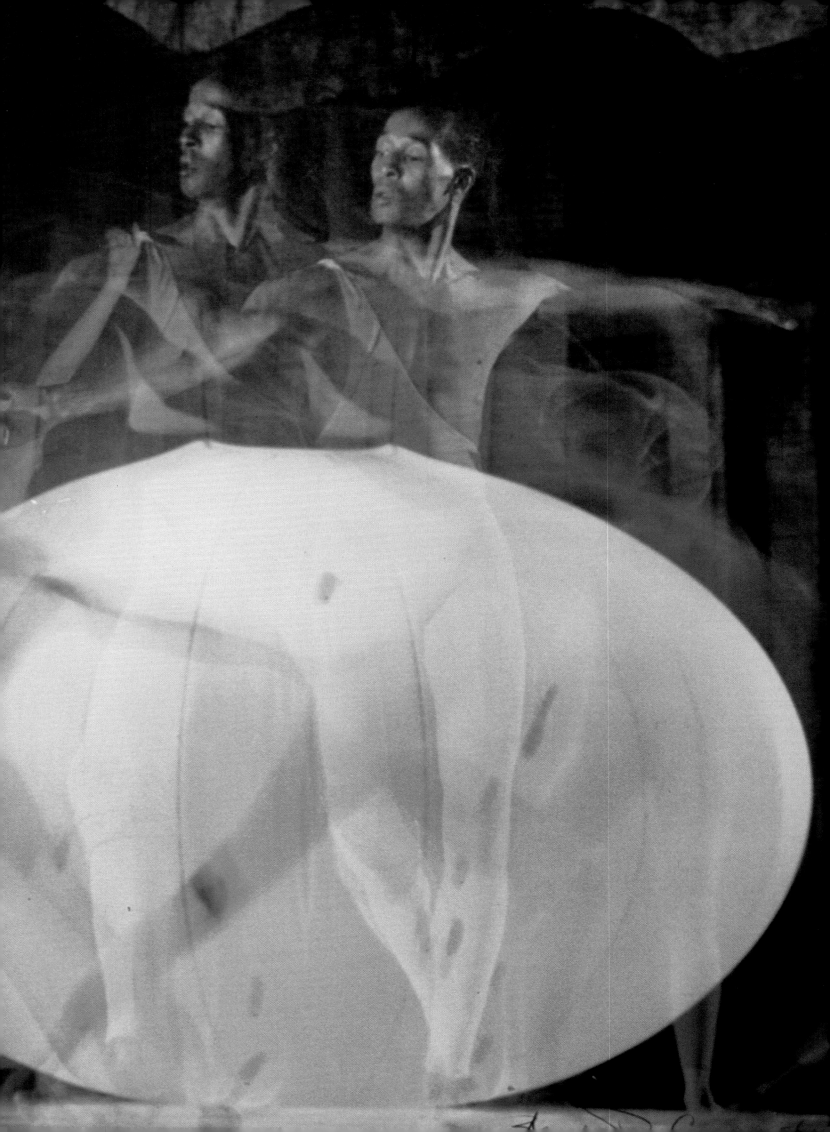

TOP: *THE NUTCRACKER* AT THE DAVID TAYLOR DANCE THEATRE, PHOTO BY DECROCE. BOTTOM LEFT: RALPH LEMON COMPANY, PHOTO BY BEATRIZ SCHILLER COURTESY OF THE COLORADO DANCE FESTIVAL. MIDDLE: ERICA MANCHA OF EL GRUPO FOLKLORICO SABOR LATINO, COURTESY EL GRUPO FOLKLORICO SABOR LATINO. BOTTOM RIGHT:THE COLORADO DANCE FESTIVAL ATTRACTS GROUPS FROM ALL OVER THE NATION. CONTRABAND IS FROM SAN FRANCISCO. COURTESY OF CIRCUIT NETWORK

EIKO AND KOMA
AT THE COLORADO DANCE FESTIVAL
PHOTO BY DAVID FULLARD

Reel Art in Denver
by M.S. Mason

Denver loves the movies. Business is booming at the local filmplex, the Denver International Film Festival is expanding from eight days to ten, the commercial film industry is growing, and it is becoming more and more possible to make a living making movies for businesses and television. The major newspapers, the *Denver Post*, the *Rocky Mountain News*, *Westword* and the *Boulder Daily Camera*, feature fine critics who stimulate interest in a variety of films, not just Hollywood blockbusters; art house cinemas boom, too. Moreover, through the film program at the University of Colorado at Boulder as well as the critical studies in film at CU-Denver, a new generation of local film-

OPENING NIGHT OF
DENVER INTERNAT
FILM FESTIVAL AT
PARAMOUNT THEA
COURTESY OF THE
DENVER MAYOR'S
OFFICE OF ART,
CULTURE AND FILM

makers is on the rise. On the Boulder campus and in enclaves around the area, members of a small group of experimental film artists are fostering the art of film in quiet, yet profoundly important ways.

One of the most important contributions to film culture in Denver is the Denver International Film Festival, now in its 18th year. Par-

EXPERIMENTAL DENVER

M.S. Mason

The University of Colorado at Boulder is home to a fine film program, anchored by award-winning film artist Stan Brakhage, renowned worldwide for his technical advances and artistic achievements. His presence in Boulder has inspired programs such as First Person Cinema at the university, a series of screenings dedicated to work made outside the Hollywood mainstream and the Hollywood standard of feature filmmaking.

Film programs at Denver's newest performance art theater, The Bug Performance & Media Art Center, also are dedicated to experimental film. Experimental filmmakers have indeed pushed the medium, exploring the technology but also pushing the boundaries of film aesthetics. Many work with found footage, creating new films out of bits and pieces of old ones, depending heavily on editing for content. Some paint directly on film or make animation by scratching forms directly on black leader. Experimental film has offered innovations such as the jump cut, solarization, the handheld camera, optical printing, advances in animation techniques and the perception that slow-motion looks soft, as well as the romantic idea that a filmmaker could be a film artist, like a poet or a painter, working as an individual with a personal vision.

But experimental films are not the only independently produced films being made in the Boulder-Denver area. Eye for an I, a festival that began in Boulder and has progressed to Denver in association with Denver International Film Society, includes animation, documentary and fiction films in its lineup. Award-winning films such as *American History* by Trey Parker and Chris Graves, and the lovely, poetic creation myth *Watunna* by Stacey Steers both won student Academy Awards and screened at Eye for an I. *Dearfield: The Road Less Traveled* by donnie l. betts, written and co-produced by TV anchor Reynelda Muse, concerns an all-black town established in Colorado early in the 20th century.

tially supported by a grant from the Scientific and Cultural Facilities District, DIFF is a noncompetitive, invitational festival dedicated to providing a platform for new independent films and the best of world cinema.

The Festival has won both the Governor's Award for Excellence in the Arts and the Mayor's Award for Excellence in the Arts. Great films are premiered at DIFF, from Woody Allen's *Crimes and Misdemeanors* to Krzysztof Kieslowski's 10-part *Decalogue* (based on the Ten Commandments) to Robert Altman's *Short Cuts*. Alan Alda, Steve Martin, Richard Dreyfuss, Rod Steiger, Gena Rowlands, Peter Falk and Lou Gossett Jr., among others, speak to audiences about their art. Important European, Asian, Latin American and American directors such as Louis Malle, Paul Cox, Wim Wenders, Bruce Beresford, Krzysztof Zanussi and Kieslowski enrich the cultural life of the region immeasurably with their films and in-person discourses on their craft.

One of the Festival's cultural strong points lies in its dedication to socially responsible art. An ongoing appreciation for Latin American, Native American and Chicano film keeps locals in touch with their neighbors. Asian and Israeli films are also sought out. Films for kids and families are part of the regular programming each year. A component called WatchFest helps keep a human rights vigil on the whole world. There is always an environmental component and a very strong documentary series. Four of the documentaries nominated for Academy Awards in 1994 were screened at DIFF and three of those qualified for nomination *because* they screened at DIFF; not all film festivals can help qualify documentaries.

A recent addition to DIFF, the New Media Festival, spotlights various media from interactive film and video, including CD-ROM and other new technology. Virtual reality, World-Wide Web and high-definition television bring all the newest technology to Denver's doorstep.

Better yet, 1995 marked the motion picture's centennial, with DIFF celebrating 100 years of movie history in grand style. Festival Director Ron Henderson invited film historians, critics and film artists to select a single film from each decade of that 100-year history, introduce the film to the audience and write about the selection for the memorial program.

Henderson and his scouts scope out the major festivals around the world to bring the best of international cinema to Denver—Cannes, Telluride, San Francisco, Sundance, Berlin, Montreal and Toronto. But DIFF also supports the best of Colorado filmmaking, which includes tributes to experimental geniuses who have contributed their technical discoveries and aesthetic brilliance to the history of film, as well as local documentarians such as Donna Dewey.

COURTESY OF MIRAMAX

COURTESY OF THE DENVER FILM SOCIETY

PHOTO BY LARRY LASZLO

Dewey, of Dewey-Obenchain Productions, has made her living in film locally for nearly 20 years. Sometimes Dewey casts out of town or brings in a first-class Hollywood cinematographer to shoot a high-profile commercial. But mostly she pulls from the local talent pools. Her commercials for McDonald's, the Colorado Lottery, Village Inn and Public Service have enjoyed heavy rotation on television. She made a documentary about gangs and is in the midst of shooting the sequel to *Homeboys*.

She also has developed a valuable network with the Hollywood and New York industries. She says getting work is much easier now than even 10 years ago because the demand for commercials has grown by leaps and bounds; it doesn't hurt that Colorado is cost effective. In addition, Denver became a viable production location when Viacom spent several years here

CLOCKWISE FROM UPPER LEFT: *Strictly Ballroom, Razor's Edge* and *The Piano* were all screened at the Denver International Film Festival

shooting the *Perry Mason* series and other productions. "When crews go back to work every day for eight years, you get very good, professional crews. In the past, crew people would have to have a second job, but because of Viacom they had the opportunity to get excellent training," Dewey says.

The Mayor's Office of Art, Culture and Film has devised a "one-stop shopping" network for out-of-state production companies, from Hollywood to New York and the international film community. Metro Denver has all those services most vital to location production. A conscientious effort has been made to husband the resources of local filmmakers, and to house, entertain and provide services for location filmmakers.

Clear, easy-to-follow filming permit rules have eradicated the threat of film productions being shut down by individual agencies. Unlike many other cities, Denver charges no fees for permits to film.

The network of professional film services has grown dramatically in the past decade—and it's all paying off. *Things to Do in Denver When You're Dead* with Andy Garcia, Treat Williams, Gabrielle Anwar and Christopher Lloyd was shot here, as was *Under Seige II: In Dark Territory,* a Warner Bros. film. In 1993 six feature films for television and six television shows (17 episodes in all) were made in Denver, including five installments of *Perry Mason*, one *Ironside* and six episodes of Dick Van Dyke's *Diagnosis Murder.*

Actors attend the Denver International Film Festival to promote their films.
TOP: Anthony Quinn received applause for *Mystique*. RIGHT: Alan Alda at the wold premiere of *The Four Seasons*. BOTTOM: D.B. Sweeney promoted *A Day in October*.

Local filmmakers have been inspired and informed by the ready availability of mainstream and art films. AMC, Mann and United Artists have dozens of screens here. The kind of intellectual stimulation that comes from viewing films from other cultures has been provided by Landmark, which has a chain of theaters throughout the West. Denver is one of its strongest markets, and eight screens provide windows into other societies and into the art of film itself.

The filmmaking community benefits from the world-class talents who share their expertise. And the love of film goes on developing in the wider community, as viewers become more sophisticated and the big screen brings the world home to Denver.

PHOTOS BY LARRY LASZLO COURTESY OF THE DENVER FILM SOCIETY

Part of *Under Siege 2: In Dark Territory* was filmed in Denver
Courtesy of the Denver Mayor's Office of Art, Culture and Film

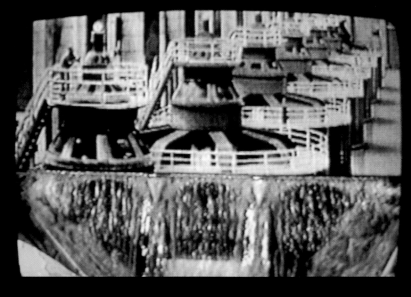

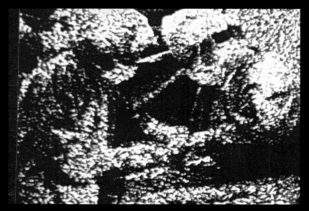

OPPOSITE PAGE: STILLS FROM *GREAT WESTERN WATER TRICK*, 17 MINUTES, 1992 BY GARY EMRICH.
ABOVE: *THE TEXT OF LIGHT* BY STAN BRAKHAGE WAS SHOT A FRAME AT A TIME, OVER A PERIOD OF SIX MONTHS, IN A GLASS ASHTRAY.
LEFT: *REMAINS TO BE SEEN* BY PHILIP SOLOMON WON FIRST PRIZE AT THE 1990 OBERHAUSSEN INTERNATIONAL FILM FESTIVAL.

Murals in the Capitol rotunda depict scenes of historical and contemporary Colorado, brought to life with quotes by former Colorado Poet Laureate Thomas Hornsby Ferril. Courtesy of the Colorado Historical Society

Water the lightning gave shall give back lightning and Men shall store the lightning for their use

literary arts

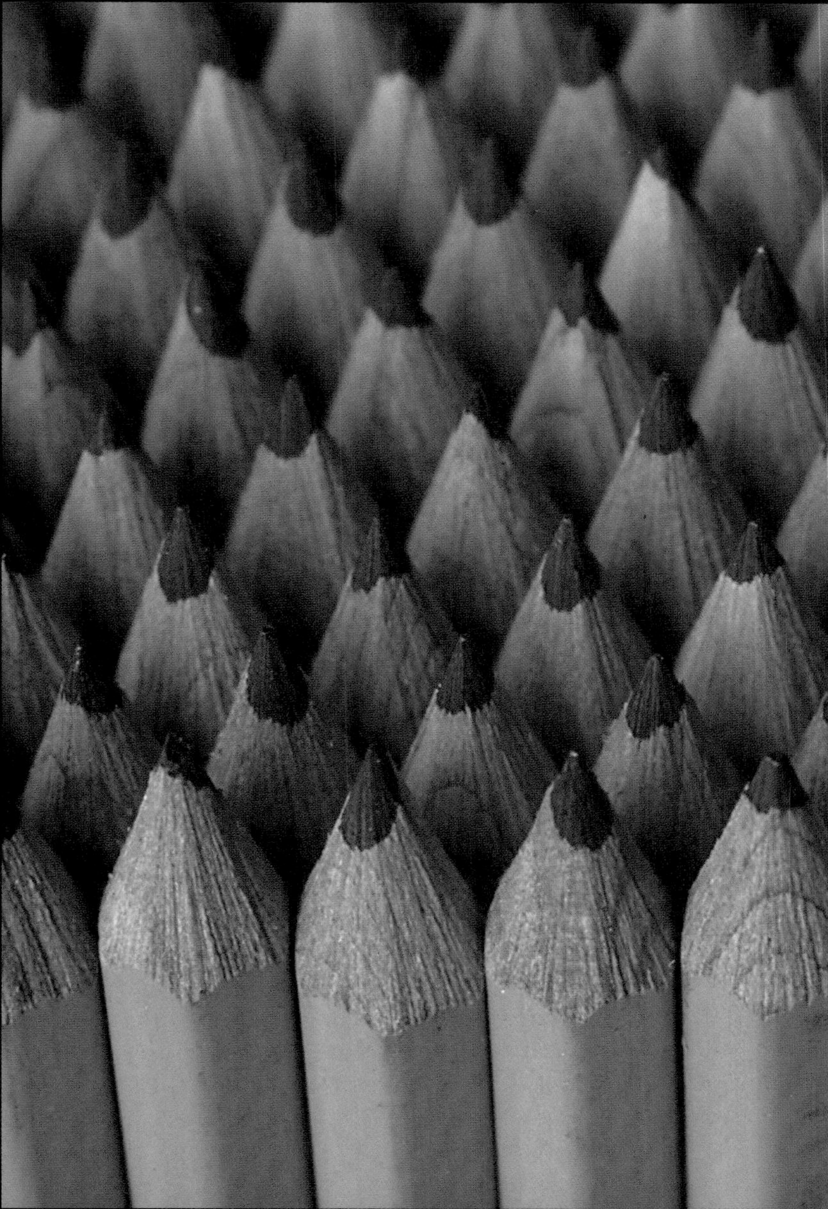

Giving us Words
by Jennifer Heath

J ack Kerouac's Denver sojourns form some of the most intense, rollicking scenes in his novel *On the Road*. The 1957 masterpiece identified the Beat Generation and broke through formal conventions to create a fresh, exuberant, passionate style of writing, completely divorced from any academy. *On the Road* was a prose accompaniment to Allen Ginsberg's poem "Howl." They were celebratory, defiant testaments to post-World War II America and helped to open a new literary era.

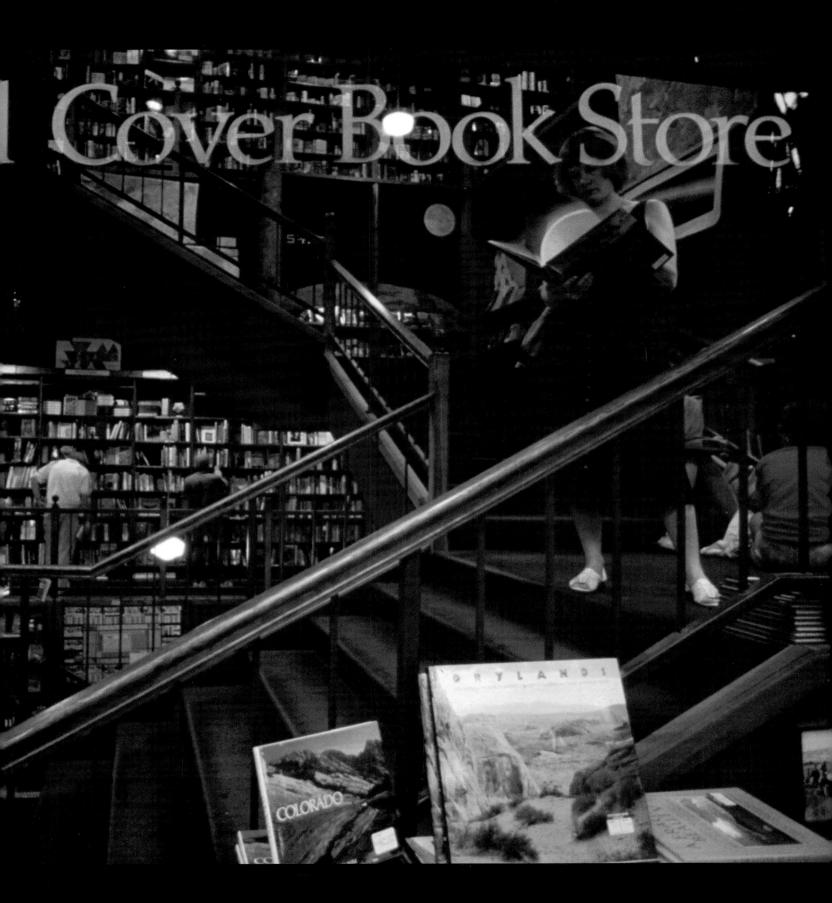

Cover Book Store

Isn't today a day men will look back upon with amazement and envy?

Seize it! Enjoy it!

———————————————

Thomas Hornsby Ferril

Five years after Kerouac's death in 1969, Ginsberg imported that explosive sensibility from New York to Colorado, when he and Anne Waldman founded the Naropa Institute's Jack Kerouac School of Disembodied Poetics in Boulder. For two decades the school has nurtured experimental writing and, summer after summer, convenes bicoastal and interna-

TOM AUER
LITERATURE IN REVIEW

Jennifer Heath

On New Year's Day 1995, editor and publisher Tom Auer told a *Rocky Mountain News* reporter he never doubted that Denver's alternative and influential literary journal, *The Bloomsbury Review*, would reach its 15th anniversary. But, he added, "I just didn't think it would feel like 50."

Tony Hillerman has called *Bloomsbury* "the best book magazine in America." It got that way, Auer says, "juggling pennies" and moonlighting, while he, his sister Marilyn and a few dedicated friends learned by trial and error how to produce a book magazine that would be a respected and unique voice for the Rocky Mountain West. The goal was "to let people know there were good books available that never made it into the *New York Times Book Review* or the *New York Review of Books*."

It began when Auer, a Denver University student working at John and Margaret Lake's Bloomsbury Books & Pool, decided to create a store newsletter to circulate around campus and the neighborhood. Within two years, Auer recalls, "the newsletter grew into a small magazine, promoting the store less, promoting books more." Soon he and his friends were "begging and borrowing" the capital to expand. Working out of Auer's home, they created a marketing plan and a production schedule. "The days were long and personal lives suffered," he says. Was it worth it? "Many dreams have been fulfilled. Many not. But the wheels are still turning."

Bloomsbury features such prestigious contributors as Wallace Stegner, Harlan Ellison, John Nichols and Edward Abbey, and is distributed throughout the United States and Canada. Certainly for the literary community, *Bloomsbury* —like its counterpart, *High Plains Literary Review*— has been invaluable. Both steadfastly support small presses and literary journals, festivals, readings and conferences; *Bloomsbury* publishes an essential *Colorado Book Guide*. *The Bloomsbury Review* and Tom Auer's tireless efforts have provided stability, a nucleus around which the Colorado literary community has been allowed to flourish.

Tom Auer, far right, back row, and the staff of the Bloomsbury Review.

tional artists, making Colorado one of the most vital centers for literature in the United States.

But even before the invasion of the Beats, there was a lively, if modest, vanguard scene cooking around the metro area. Poet Jack Collom, author of *Blue Heron & IBC* and *Arguing With Something Plato Said*, recalls that "in the '60s, an influx of poets from California arrived

and connected up with Denver poets to form a sort of minimalist, keen but scruffy street-poet corps. Among them were Jimmy Ryan Morris, Tony Scibella, Larry Lake and Stuart Z. Perkoff. The Black Ace Bookstore was a hangout.

"As Naropa entered the scene, so, simultaneously, other energetic literary movements burgeoned on other fronts. On one hand, interesting young poets like Reed Bye, Marc Campbell and Marilyn Krysl emerged from the woodwork, while the University of Colorado began hiring active, alternative poets and writers such as Ed Dorn, Ron Sukenick, Steve Katz, Peter Michelson and playwright Sidney Goldfarb."

Marilyn Krysl remains a stalwart of the Denver metro literary scene as the poetry editor of the University of Colorado at Boulder's prestigious *Many Mountains Moving* literary review, edited by Naomi Horii. Meanwhile, longtime college professors Reg Saner, a Walt Whitman poetry prize recipient, and Rex Burns, author of the popular Gabe Wagner mysteries, have danced steadily, imperturbably, through every change and hullabaloo.

The expansion from regionalism into the world at large seemed to climax in 1994 when the University of Colorado sponsored The Novel of the Americas, a huge celebration, organized by Professor Ray Williams, of diverse writers from every conceivable ethnic background throughout the Western Hemisphere.

The Novel of the Americas also reflected the rise in the '60s of the Mexican-American movement, La Raza, which saw a rush of Chicano poets distinguished for activist art that challenged the status quo in a demand for social justice. The verse of Ray Gonzalez, Lorna Dee Cervantes and Abelardo Delgado—recipient of a Denver Mayor's Award for Excellence in the Arts—digs deep into the roots of Latino literary traditions, a hybrid of Native American, Spanish and European-American poetic patterns.

Denver is younger than a white-haired man
Remembering yellow gold up to the grass roots
They tell of eagles older than Denver is.
—Thomas Hornsby Ferril

Amid the literary foment and influx of the avant-garde, Thomas Hornsby Ferril held the line for graceful, old-fashioned dignity, formality and erudition. Considered by some the West's foremost poet, Ferril was born in Denver in 1896, the son of a pioneer newsman. He worked as a reporter for the old *Denver Times* and the *Rocky Mountain News* before becoming a press agent for Great Western Sugar Co. Poet and historian Carl Sandburg, his friend, described Ferril as "terrifically and beautifully American." His volumes, including *Westering*, *Anvil of Roses*, *High Passage* and *Words for Denver and Other Poems*, are now Western poetry classics.

In 1979 Governor Dick Lamm named Ferril Colorado poet laureate. Of the many honors presented him—and they were myriad—one could speculate that the Robert Frost poetry award was one of his most prized. The famous New Englander paid tribute to Ferril in verse: "I know a Denverite/Who, measured from sea to crown,/is one mile five-foot-ten/And he swings a commensurate pen."

Ferril died in 1988, the last and most eminent of Colorado's poets laureate. Nine inscriptions of his poetry illuminate a series of murals in the state capitol rotunda.

Unlike many other Colorado-born writers of that period, Ferril was to stay here. Many who

READINGS: POETRY OUT LOUD
Jennifer Heath

For centuries, public eating and drinking establishments have served as literary venues, but in the late 20th century the custom has seemed to tumble into the dusty past along with beatniks and bongos. These days, however, it's nearly impossible to sit down for a contemplative cup of coffee without encountering a poetry and/or prose reading.

The Denver Press Club has been a steady—and sometimes the only—outlet since 1894. Poets Ed Ward and Woody Hildebrandt took the lead in the late 1960s and early '70s by arranging intermittent readings at hot spots such as the Mercury Cafe and Muddy's Java Cafe. Seven years ago poet Tom Peters began producing "So You're A Poet!" at Boulder's Penny Lane Coffeehouse. It was the first reguiar weekly series and features invited writers as well as an open reading. Peters has never missed a single Monday night.

Public libraries and bookstores, of course, are vital links on the circuit. The Tattered Cover, Hue Man Experience Bookstore, the Book Garden in Denver and the Boulder Bookstore—to name a few—all host writers of varying genre and fame.

The startling revival of poetry as popular art in the Denver metro area is, in large measure, nourished by the conscientious offices of Catherine O'Neill, producer of the "Toads in the Garden" reading series and editor of *Poiesis*, a bimonthly newsletter and calendar of events. At last count more than 30 locations, including theaters, taverns and art galleries, sponsor readings.

One can be uplifted, enlightened and entertained by the rhythms and ruminations of individual readers or psychically assaulted by slam poets, performance bards who compete in the ancient Celtic and Norse traditions and whose "winners" are determined by audience response. By contrast, the annual Sumo Haiku Heavyweight Championship, presented by writer Tree Bernstein, determines by rounds, like a wrestling match with professional-poet judges, the best area practitioners of this delicate and venerable three-line Japanese verse form.

did not emigrate toward the bright lights of Hollywood or New York have been all but forgotten, except in the hearts of Western-lore devotees. Once again, however, the focus on place has come into vibrant context in the works of Colorado writers, ranging from Native American authors such as poet/novelist Linda Hogan to Ohio transplant Merrill Gilfillan, whose contem-

LUIS ALBERTO URREA

Jennifer Heath

It is said that the essence of the Chicano experience lies in ambiguity. The undulating borders between cultures—at once smothering and liberating—are where Luis Alberto Urrea locates his marvelously cinematic poetry and prose.

For Urrea, who was born in Tijuana in 1955, the cultural, social, emotional and geographical frontiers were made all the more confusing by the fact that he is a *guerito*, the light-skinned child of an Anglo mother and Mexican father. The barbed wire and *migras*, the barrios where he grew up, the longing, resentment and poverty, and the racism and hatred within his own family contribute to the ferocious depth, wit and tension in his highly acclaimed books *In Search of Snow*, *The Fever of Being* (which won the 1994 Western States Book Award for poetry) and *Across the Wire: Life and Hard Times on the Mexican Border*. The pain of his experiences growing up, Urrea told one interviewer, is repeatedly exorcised through his books. "Most everything I write ends up being tragicomic. Even when I don't mean to, I often write the saddest comedies in town."

Now living in Boulder, Urrea graduated from the University of California-San Diego in 1977 and in 1982 taught expository writing at Harvard. In 1993, having won various awards and been published widely in magazines and anthologies, he burst onto the mainstream literary scene with his three books, which were greeted with wild accolades from *The New York Times*, *The Los Angeles Times* and other prestigious literary reviews.

"The silence that was neither Spanish nor English was my prayer," Urrea writes of the space he has struggled to inhabit between warring worlds. **"And God was good: there came no sound until morning."**

Luis Alberto Urrea
with the subjects of his first
book, *Across the Wire*.

plative, observant *Magpie Rising* and *Sworn Before Cranes* have received high national acclaim, to writers of modern Westerns like Steven Overholser and Terry Johnson.

"Colorado has a rich, lost history of authors who were born here and left," says poet Tom Peters, proprietor of Boulder's Beat Bookshop and possessor of a wealth of literary history. He

PHOTO BY JOHN LUEDERS-BOOTH

notes that Ken Kesey and Jean Stafford are among native Coloradans, as was Dalton Trumbo, author of *Johnny Get Your Gun*, who suffered the notorious cruelties of McCarthyism and was blacklisted with the so-called "Hollywood 10." In 1993, years after his death, students at the University of Colorado, Trumbo's alma mater, named a fountain after him in an attempt to restore his libeled reputation.

John Fante was born in Boulder in 1909. The life story of the author of *Brotherhood of the Grape*, *West of Rome* and *Ask the Dust* somewhat exemplifies the writer-exodus of the times. As a boy, Peters says, Fante envisioned a plaque to himself and his fictional baseball-hero character, Bandini, installed at the public library, but no such honor has been bestowed. In his quest for recognition, Fante left Colorado and was "discovered" in Los Angeles when his correspondence with Baltimore newspaper columnist H.L. Mencken was published. The "discovery" made Fante the "most famous busboy in America." Mild infamy also arrived with the publication of *1933 Was a Bad Year* before he went on to write the screenplay *Walk on the Wild Side*. He died in 1983 before his novel *Wait Until*

Spring, Bandini was finally made into a film produced by Francis Ford Coppola. It is said that Fante rarely visited his home state.

Things have changed drastically. With fax machines and modems, communicating with publishing centers and the outside world grows infinitely easier, and the Denver area has become far more sophisticated and urbane. Thanks to support from the Colorado Council on the Arts and various other funding agencies, thanks to the encouragement and succor of an increasingly strong literary community, there is less need for writers to leave Colorado. The Front Range has become a mecca for poets and prose writers, who not only stay but arrive en masse, attracted by the intellectual as well as physical climate. Calling Colorado home are exciting young writers such as Nicolas Samaras, Colorado Book Award and Yale Younger Poets Award winner; Luis Alberto Urrea, recipient of the 1994 Western States Book Award; experimental novelist Mark Amerika, author of *The Kafka Chronicles* and publisher of *Alternative X*, an experimental literary anthology on World Wide Net; psycho-thriller author Stephen White, author of *Privileged Information*; Seth, a riveting African-American performance poet; and many, many others.

The Colorado Center for the Book, which is affiliated with the Library of Congress Center for the Book, champions literature in Denver. Its annual Rocky Mountain Book Festival brings 300 authors and 100 exhibitors to more than 40,000 literary denizens.

A testimony to the seriousness of Colorado's literary renaissance is a recent campaign, spearheaded by *The Bloomsbury Review* editor Tom Auer, poet Catherine O'Neill and *Rocky Mountain News* writer John Enslin, to reinstate the position of Colorado poet laureate, an honorary office that had been filled spottily at best and was abandoned altogether when Ferril died.

Jack Kerouac might have been dubious of the effort, but Thomas Hornsby Ferril would have been profoundly pleased.

It's hard to housebreak a chicken.
They just don't make very good pets.
You might teach one bird imitations
But that's 'bout as good as it gets.
—*Baxter Black*

POETRY RODEO
Jennifer Heath

Despite our protestations, Denverites are reminded of our cow-town roots every year. In April the Denver Poetry Rodeo, featuring 12 straight hours of poetic marathon, gallops into town, supplied with enough versifying to tame the wildest sonnet, though the artistry is not necessarily Western-bent nor *vaquero*-oriented.

In January, when the National Western Stock Show stampedes into the city with real wranglers and rodeos, broncos and buckeroos, and home-home-on-the-range ambience, the Arvada Center for the Arts and Humanities celebrates Western life and lineage with a gathering of cowboy poets who maintain an oral tradition that, until six years ago, few people were aware existed among the corrals and cattle drives.

The Colorado Cowboy Poetry Gathering is first on the bronco versifiers' circuit. After Arvada they take off for Elko, Nevada, where as many as 10,000 cowboys and cowgals convene to hear Robert Service-style rhymes and high-class yodeling that even features Australian and Hawaiian cowbards.

Chief among the Colorado cowboy poets is Baxter Black, a veterinarian from Brighton with a bandido moustache and the wit and wisdom of a Shakespeare-on-the-plains. But Colorado also boasts such renowned rhymers as Hank Real Bird, Maggie Sharp, John Schaffner, Tim Nolting, Chuck Pyle, the Pfeiffer Brothers, Bob Huff and Liz Masterson, many of whom are more, well, musically than literarily bent. Word among the cowboy poets is that Colorado is strong on talent.

Vess Quinlan, a cowboy poet who farms near Alamosa and is largely responsible for organizing the Arvada gathering, says that cowboys have always written poetry and loved Shakespeare as much as Service. Created by everyone from black cowpokes to Italian, Dutch or Irish immigrant ranch hands and the surplus sons of English lords, cowboy poems were regularly printed in 19th-century cattlemen's periodicals or simply collected by word of mouth around the campfire. Over time they were appended and altered but never forgotten.

For all the nostalgia, these maverick poets are respected by the bardic establishment. Their rootin' tootin' rhymes can be read between the lines.

STEPHEN WHITE, AUTHOR OF *PRIVILEGED INFORMATION*
AND *PRIVATE PRACTICES.*   PHOTO BY GARY ISAACS

LINDA HOGAN, NOVELIST.   PHOTO BY GARY ISAACS

ALLEN GINSBERG, POET. PHOTO BY GRANT LEDUC
COURTESY OF THE NAROPA INSTITUTE

BAXTER BLACK, COWBOY POET. PHOTO BY GARY ISAACS

RAY GONZALEZ, POET   PHOTO BY GARY ISAACS

KEN KESEY, AUTHOR OF *SAILOR SONG*

© BRIAN LANKER.

ABOVE: POET JACK COLLOM
COURTESY OF JACK COLLOM

ABOVE RIGHT: ALLEN GINSBERG, GREGORY CORSO,
WILLIAM BURROUGHS AND ANNE WALDMAN
COURTESY OF THE NAROPA INSTITUTE

LEFT: POET ANNE WALDMAN
COURTESY OF THE NAROPA INSTITUTE

Young Artists' Eyes
by Jennifer Heath

The surest way to corrupt a [child] is to teach him to esteem more highly those who think alike than those who think differently. —Frederich Nietzsche

Without the arts, children are destined for pinched imaginations and arrested intellects. In a world dominated by mainstream media, where kids often are spoon fed vapid, conflicting or mean-spirited information, the arts are a saving grace that enhance analytical skills, broaden appreciation of diversity, improve self-discipline and communication, and offer a means to clarity and self-esteem. The classic "three R's" of education—reading, 'riting and 'rithmetic— are not adequate to introduce a human mind to its full potential.

Sixth- through 9th-grade students must audition for Denver Public Schools' School of the Arts, where they are exposed to intensive multicultural training in creative writing, theater, visual arts, dance and music. The students attend Cole Middle School and Manuel High School for their academic courses. Performance is stressed, but, perhaps more important, process is emphasized to prepare children not only for potential careers in the arts but to give them appreciation and enjoyment of and a safe harbor in art throughout their lives. Whether they grow up to become actors, musicians or businesspeople, butchers, bakers or sculpture makers, their lives will always be profoundly informed and graced by their foundations in the arts.

To ensure "that the arts are a part of every Colorado child's education" is the guiding principle of Young Audiences, founded in 1963. It presents teacher training, educational performances, arts tours and a wide-ranging artists-in-residence program in collaboration with the Colorado Council on the Arts.

"Blue!" "Santa Claus!" "Orange!" "My dog!" "My dad!" "The key of G!"

Little hands wave, vying for attention. Laughter, delight, curiosity in bloom. Eyes wide and glowing. Fresh ideas and enlightenment enter the classroom with a visiting artist, poet, musician, storyteller or dancer. Navigators into the unknown.

"Dude!" "Rad!"

Young Mr. or Ms. Cool is suddenly profoundly impressed by what he or she has discovered can be accomplished. Classroom teachers in traditional public schools struggle heroically to nourish students and meet their curricular needs, yet without the visiting artist it might never have occurred to this teenager that he or she could write a poem, choreograph a dance or contribute some important element to a collaborative work of art such as a mural.

Year after year in thousands of classrooms, despite disappearing arts budgets in public schools, Young Audiences fuels creativity and expands the spirit. Its leadership has inspired myriad large and small arts and science organizations, from the Ars Nova Chamber Singers to El Centro Su Teatro, from the African-American Moyo Nguvu Cultural Arts Center to the Birds of Prey Rehabilitation Foundation, all of whom make their skills and services available to schools. The philosophies of these groups are similar to those of Young Audiences and they frequently act in tandem with the schools.

The Denver metro area boasts some of the finest children's museums and cultural venues in the nation. Activities abound. Denver's renowned Paramount Theatre has offered a "Children are Paramount" program featuring live multidisciplinary presentations, by national and international touring groups, of drama classics, dance and movement productions or simple entertainment.

The annual Historic Denver Week customarily begins with a "Box City Project," in which

"Wynken, Blynken and Nod" (Detail) by Mabel Landrum Torrey.

COURTESY OF DENVER PUBLIC LIBRARY WESTERN HISTORY DEPARTMENT

A POET AND A DREAMER

Jennifer Heath

Eugene Field is the poet laureate of children throughout the English-speaking world. A newspaperman and editor of the *Denver Tribune* from 1881 to 1883, Field wrote reams of nearly forgotten Western poetry and some of the most enduring children's verse ever put to paper. To this day, parents read or recite "The Gingham Dog and the Calico Cat," "Night Wind," "The Sugar-Plum Tree," "The Duel" and, most beloved of all, "The Dutch Lullaby," now known as "Wynken, Blynken and Nod."

In 1881 Field and his family moved to Denver to a small house on West Colfax Avenue. His own progeny numbered eight, but three died in childhood. The concluding lines of "Little Boy Blue" describe those heartaches.

Yet for all the sorrow expressed in the poem, Field was a joyful and humorous man, a practical joker who brought genial grief to his *Tribune* readers (and his competition at the *Rocky Mountain News*) through his daily satirical column, "Odd Gossip." He is said to have had the open heart and frank nature of a child, and he loved nothing better than to be surrounded by youngsters, singing songs and telling stories.

Although Field died in 1898 in Chicago, he is so revered by Coloradans and so thoroughly adopted by Denver that his West Colfax cottage was repaired and moved to Washington Park as a memorial. Nearby is a marble statue, created in the 1920s by Mabel Landrum Torrey, of Wynken, Blynken and Nod—three sweet, bedazzled figures sailing through dreams in a shoe. The piece is part of the Collection of the City and County of Denver.

children, with the help of the Denver Chapter of the American Institute of Architects, design and construct cardboard buildings, setting them on a city grid. "Box City" gives children experience in city planning and urban development, insight into how they, as adults, will choose to shape their own communities. Meanwhile, groups such as the Thorne Ecological Institute conduct sum-

mer outings that match children with artists for outdoor nature and art excursions.

The Children's Museum of Denver is a marvelous bit of architectural whimsy. The museum was established in 1973 with a seed grant from the Junior League of Denver. Its turqoise and pink building houses permanent installations as well as traveling exhibitions: a display of origi-

COURTESY OF KAY NEGASH

Kay Negash of the Rocky Mountain Storyteller's Guild.

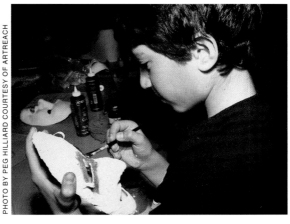

PHOTO BY PEG HILLIARD COURTESY OF ARTREACH

PHOTO BY JEAN CASBARIAN COURTESY OF ARTREACH

MARJORIE GOLDSTEIN
ACCESS TO ART

Jennifer Heath

Marjorie Goldstein has spent a lifetime in service to others. Since the mid-80s she has been executive director of ArtReach. Before that she was director of volunteer services for Mile High United Way. ArtReach encompasses two of her greatest passions: culture and the well-being of humanity.

A self-proclaimed "frustrated artist"—"I go to the Denver Art Students League in disguise," she quips—Goldstein received a degree in sociology from the University of Denver.

Until she began working with minority groups, Goldstein says, she had "no clue of real hardships. I saw another side of life and I wanted to get people together to solve problems. At ArtReach we are not independent, we always have to adapt to what's going on in the community."

ArtReach was started in 1974 and serves more than 70,000 people a year, primarily high-risk kids and their families. Yet the roster also includes recent immigrants, mentally and physically challenged people, prisoners and the elderly, "who have been terribly isolated."

By cooperating with a network of 250 non-profit organizations, "ArtReach is able to bring arts to many people who've had no experience whatsoever. They've never been to a play, never been to the zoo. At one of our six-week workshops, the kids had never even had paper or crayons. We added an extra six weeks to the program just to give the children time to feel out those most basic tools before we continued."

Goldstein recalls that when her family moved from Denver to Dallas for a few years, she attended an exhibition and sale of prisoners' artwork. "I was so homesick for Colorado, and I saw a beautiful painting of pine trees and the mist and the mountains. This prisoner had created the same wonderful vision that I could not get out of my mind. I still have the painting in my office today."

nal illustrations from Tomie de Paola's magnificent books, *Strega Nona* and *The Art Lesson*, or an exhibit of 600 creations by Jefferson County students working in literature, music, photography and the visual arts.

An entire wing of the museum is dedicated to science, with elaborate interactive learning spaces. As art and science become increasingly

COURTESY OF OPALANGA PUGH

OPALANGA PUGH
THE POWER OF A STORY

Jennifer Heath

Six feet tall, gap-toothed and endowed with a glorious voice, storyteller Opalanga Pugh presents a beautiful, imposing figure as she thrills and teaches her audiences with tales about Sojourner Truth, Winnie Mandela and High John, or with legends of bush medicine and futuristic myths. A two-time recipient of the Denver Mayor's Award for Excellence in the Arts, Pugh's repertoire of profound and alchemical tales include African, African-American, Native American, Asian and Hispanic folklore.

As a gangly teenager growing up in mostly white Denver, Pugh suffered an awkward adolescence and the deep oppression felt by outsiders. Even the gap in her front teeth was labeled the mark of a liar. A sojourn in West Africa during her senior year in college liberated her. There she found that tall, gap-toothed women are revered as lucky and fecund. She also discovered the *griot* tradition, the African storyteller/healer who gives a non-preaching voice to problems and can therefore solve them. Back in Colorado, Pugh tackled Hans Christian Andersen's classic *The Ugly Duckling*. The process of rephrasing the tale of a scorned and rejected creature into a new, African-American rendition allowed Pugh herself to transform, like the wretched little duckling, into a proud, magnificent swan.

Today Pugh is an internationally acclaimed performer, often collaborating with dancers, musicians and vocalists. She is a wise and loving "edu-trainer" who conducts seminars throughout the country in order to "reveal the power of story," she says, "in balancing human potential and technology as we enter the 21st century."

In class and concert, Pugh offers powerful messages of hope and healing to adults as well as children. She is an artist who believes in "universal wisdom," and that stories, as Nigerian author Chinua Achebe said, "are not just meant to make us smile . . . our very lives depend on them."

intertwined (as, indeed, they were even in Leonardo da Vinci's day), these kinds of activities lead to a deeper understanding of the world. A recent traveling show, *Circus of Circles*, was a dynamic environment where young visitors could investigate the ubiquity of roundness: patterns in art and architecture, mandalas, gears, tops and circles created in nature and on comput-

COURTESY OF YOUNG AUDIENCES

COURTESY OF YOUNG AUDIENCES

Young Audiences brought artists Gwylym Cano of El Centro Su Teatro (top), Bob Hall (above) and Lindy Soon Curry (right) to elementary audiences.

ers. A workshop by *Anti-Coloring Book* author Susan Striker helped focus the exhibit and gave children additional ways to solve problems and think critically.

In Boulder a much smaller yet increasingly vibrant space, Collage Children's Museum, strives along the same paths, with a calendar chock-full of intriguing cross-cultural dance, art, poetry, storytelling and crafts events.

One of the best-kept secrets in the area is the children's room in the basement of the University of Colorado-Boulder Museum, where little ones can explore the inner workings of earth, plants and animals or "try on" other cultures. The Denver Art Museum's Kids Corner and its Learning to Look and Saturdays for Families tours are constantly crowded with children and their parents, all enchanted by the magical history of art.

While touring the Arvada Center for the Arts and Humanities' museum and art gallery, one

COURTESY OF YOUNG AUDIENCES

can be treated to a variety of impromptu mini-concerts. Young jazz dancers or tiny ballerinas can-can or pirouette behind the glass wall of a mirrored studio. Upstairs the theater is buzzing. More than 60,000 children a year attend Arvada's diverse dramas.

The play's the thing at Arvada, with no fewer than 35 acting and dance classes for youth listed in the fall catalog. And there are historical participation plays such as *The Mystery of Rebekeh* and *The Ghost of the Haine's Log House*, which take place in the standing remains of Arvada's pioneer days.

The center also presents a wealth of other arts and outreach programs: puppetry; kite-making; collage; ceramics; painting; drawing; writing; juggling; an interdisciplinary, introductory arts class for preschoolers; a charming youth symphony; and a children's chorus.

It is an immeasurable joy to see and hear youngsters throw themselves into the arts with such devotion, fun and determination. It is equally astonishing to experience the performances of Denver's 100-piece Young Artists Orchestra or the Colorado Children's Chorale, an internationally traveled and acclaimed vocal

STORYTELLER ANGEL VIGIL

Jennifer Heath

Angel Vigil has devoted a lifetime to kids and *cuentos* (tales). Now chair of the Fine and Performing Arts Department and director of drama at Colorado Academy, his fruitful career has spanned every facet of theater, from ballet to playwriting. A recipient of the Colorado Governor's Award for Excellence in Education and the Denver Mayor's Individual Artist Fellowship, Vigil is a master storyteller who has helped to bring Hispanic *cuentos* into the lives of children throughout the state. His recent book, *The Corn Mother and Other Legends and Stories of the Hispanic Southwest*, includes the following charming tale:

> *Like Father, Like Son*
> *(De Tal Palo, Tal Astilla)*

Once there was a family that consisted of the father, the mother, the grandpa and the little child. The grandpa had lived with his son, the father of the family, for many years. His wife, the grandma of the family, had died during an especially hard winter long ago. When his wife died, the grandpa was thankful that he had a son with whom he could live. As the years passed and he grew older, he especially enjoyed the company of his grandson.

During the years when he was younger, the grandpa was able to help with the chores of running the farm. During these years, he was active in the life of the family, and he felt he had a place in his son's home.

With the passing of the years, however, he grew ill and was not able to help with the work on the farm. Gradually, he was able to do less and less. The wife started to complain that the grandpa was nothing but work and maybe they should think about getting him to live someplace else.

The son did not want to send his father away, but then he thought, "Maybe my wife is right. He is not much use anymore, and he might be happier somewhere else." He called his young son over and said, "Go get a blanket and put it in the barn for your grandpa. He is old and useless, so he is moving to the barn."

The young son got the blanket and then got a pair of scissors and started to cut the blanket in two.

The father asked the boy, "What are you doing? That is a perfectly good blanket."

The boy answered his father, "I am cutting the blanket in two pieces so when you get old like grandpa, I will have a blanket to give you when you move into the barn."

From that day on the grandpa continued to live in the house with the family.

assembly with six choirs comprised of 400 children from throughout Denver and the surrounding communities.

When more and more youngsters are in jeopardy, when gangs ravage cities across the country, and poverty and alienation undermine children's lives, groups such as ArtReach and Barrio ArtCry are pivotal.

LEARNING ALIVE

Jennifer Heath

COURTESY OF YOUNG AUDIENCES

There is nothing artist-in-residence Kristine Smock says she gives children that she doesn't get back twofold.

"The kids teach me patience and compassion. They loosen me up for my own artwork and remind me about my place in the universe," she says.

Known to administrators and teachers as one of the area's most inspiring and inventive visiting artists, Smock, a ceramist and sculptor, began working with youngsters through Young Audiences' residency program in the late '80s. For an independent project she titled "Forest Through the Trees," Smock organized about 100 children of varying ages to make large sculptures "vaguely in the form of trees," entirely from recycled materials. They invaded trash barrels and dumpsters and saved their soda pop cans, then displayed their creations at a local gallery. In the process they learned about both art and the environment.

"Building art," Smock says, "is about building community and looking at the planet in a holistic way. In my classes we talk a lot about self-respect and cooperation."

She works mainly with clay, "a totally natural medium for kids. It's full, it's earth, where we come from, what we walk on, where we eventually go."

One of her roles is to make manifest whatever subject children are being taught. Her groups have built Native American shelters and studied the pottery of indigenous peoples. They've formed African and Latin American percussive instruments and then presented concerts. They've shaped animals, built birdhouses and feeders, and even "mummified" their stuffed toys for an Egyptian study unit.

"I try to figure out ways to open the kids' minds and bodies to new things. So many kids are frightened—some first-graders refuse to draw because they're afraid of not being perfect. It's my job to teach them to take risks and be as crazy and wacky with their imaginations as they can."

One mission of organizations such as ArtReach and Barrio ArtCry is to instill children with respect for and knowledge of all ethnic traditions, especially pride in their own.

ArtReach's Culture for Kids, Art on the Edges and other projects bring art to economically disadvantaged and emotionally disturbed youngsters through field trips, workshops and performances produced at human service agencies or in community centers.

Barrio ArtCry was developed by youngsters themselves almost as a kind of club. Chicano teens focus on their heritage in theater, creative writing, video production, mural making and even a Schwinn "lo-bikes" adaptation of the Chicano "low-rider" folk art tradition.

These activities have been fostered by, among others, ArtReach, the Hunt Alternatives Fund and the Chicano Humanities and Arts Council, and "parented" by professional Hispanic artists such as Rick Manzanares, Maruca Salazar, Anthony Ortega, Meggan Rodriguez and Carlos Fresquez.

Perhaps because artists perceive themselves to be outriders in society, they are customarily generous with time and energy. Cleo Parker Robinson— who 25 years ago founded one of the nation's few African-American dance troupes—has evolved Project Self-Discovery, which has brought some 25,000 youngsters under its wing with a view toward art as an alternative to peer pressure and substance abuse.

The Rocky Mountain Storyteller's Guild, spearheaded by Kay Negash, recently received substantial funding from the Scientific and Cultural Facilities District to tell stories in teen detention facilities. Negash and other tellers visit the jails where, she notes, "storytelling works because nothing is asked of how they hear and interpret the stories. You can see tense, wound-up children slowly unwind into a state of relaxed intimacy."

That's the key: Art creates intimacy with oneself, which in turn is empowering, a personal adventure that leads toward wholeness.

A student with the mask she created at a
Boulder Action for Soviet Jewry workshop with
artist Peg Hilliard. The children created masks
and characters for a story about each one.
photo by Peg Hilliard courtesy of ArtReach

COLORADO BALLET DANCERS
MINGLE WITH ADAMS COUNTY
SCHOOLCHILDREN AFTER A
PERFORMANCE OF *SLEEPING
BEAUTY* AT THE TEMPLE HOYNE
BUELL THEATRE.
PHOTO BY TERRY SHAPIRO
COURTESY OF ARTREACH

165

TOP: COLORADO CHILDREN'S CHORALE
PHOTO BY LARRY LASZLO

RIGHT: ARTIST CARLOTTA ESPINOZA TAUGHT
A VISUAL ARTS WORKSHOP AT CURTIS PARK
COMMUNITY CENTER. THIS YOUNG ARTIST IS
WORKING ON A MURAL.
PHOTO BY JEAN CASBARIAN
COURTESY OF ARTREACH

Art *Ensemble*
by Elizabeth Emmett

T he creative force behind a painting, photograph, a dance or a poem is a powerful thing; bring several or even hundreds of artists together and you've got a virtuoso juggernaut that can't help but affect those present.

In Denver, citizens delight in art and artists at more than 100 festivals and related events each year. The Colorado Performing Arts Festival, the Capitol Hill People's Fair and the Cherry Creek Arts Festival, as well as smaller celebrations of specific genres, passions or styles, let Denverites nurture, very publicly, their remarkable legacy of art, culture and diversity.

PHOTO BY JAMES A. ROE
COURTESY OF DOWNTOWN DENVER PARTNERSHIP

PHOTO BY
TODD LANGLEY
COURTESY OF
CHERRY CREEK ARTS
FESTIVAL

TOP LEFT: The annual NEWS4 Parade of Lights, held the first weekend in December, draws more than 300,000 revelers to witness the spectacular arrival of Santa's sleigh. TOP MIDDLE: Against the backdrop of the state Capitol, crowds gather in the Greek Amphitheater to hear some of the area's hottest bands during the two-day Capitol Hill People's Fair. TOP RIGHT: July's annual AT&T LoDo Music Festival has become the most popular weekend of music in Denver. Here, the funky sounds of War echo across Coors Field and Union Station. LEFT: The Cherry Creek Arts Festival features more than 200 of the nation's finest visual artists. Accessibility Hour provides a special viewing time for differently abled people. ABOVE: Cinco de Mayo on Santa Fe kicks off this Mexican holiday with performers, demonstrations and vendors from Colorado's Hispanic and Latino communities. PHOTO © BUZZ MORRISON

"Colorado Thunderhead"
from *Cloud Series* by
Mark Sink

These local groups receive support from the Scientific and Cultural Facilities District.

Adams County Historical Society
Alternative Arts Alliance
Arapahoe County Springfest, Inc.
Arapahoe Philharmonic Suite
Ars Nova Chamber Singers
Art Students League of Denver
ArtReach
Arts Communications, Inc.
Arts & Humanities Assembly of Boulder
Arts Studio, Inc.
Arvada Center for the Arts & Humanities
Arvada Historical Society
Asian American Foundation of Colorado
Asian Art Coordinating Council
Asian Cultural Center Suite
Astor House Hotel Museum
Aurora Arts & Humanities Council
Aurora Dance Arts
Aurora Fox Arts Center
Aurora History Museum
Aurora Potters Guild
Aurora Visual Arts
Ballet Denver Co.
Birds of Prey Rehabilitation Foundation
Black American West Museum
Boulder Art Association
Boulder Art Center
Boulder Bach Festival
Boulder Ballet Ensemble
Boulder Coounty Folk & Bluegrass Association
Boulder Concert Band, Inc.
Boulder County Nature Association
Boulder Dance Alliance
Boulder Friends of Jazz
Boulder Historical Society
Boulder Native Plant Society
Boulder Philharmonic Orchestra
Boulder Postoley Dance Ensemble
Boulder Repertory Company
Boulder Songmakers
Boulder Theatre Producers Guild
Boulder Timberliners Barbershop Chorus
Boulder Youth Symphony Society
Broomfield Civic Orchestra
Broomfield Council on the Arts & Humanities
Broomfield Depot Museum
Buffalo Bill Memorial Museum
Cantabile Singers
Centennial Philharmonic
Center for Creative Arts Therapy
Central City Opera
Changing Scene
Cherry Creek Arts Festival
Cherry Creek Chorale
Chicano Humanities & Arts Council
Children's Museum of Denver
CityStage
Cleo Parker Robinson Dance Theatre
Collage Children's Museum
Colorado Aviation Historical Society
Colorado Ballet
Colorado Bird Observatory
Colorado Celtic Dance Association
Colorado Chautauqua Association
Colorado Children's Chorale
Colorado Chorale
Colorado Dance Alliance
Colorado Dance Festival
Colorado Dramatists
Colorado Educational Theatre, Inc.
Colorado Federation of the Arts
Colorado Grange Museum
Colorado Honor Band Association
Colorado Irish Pipe Band
Colorado Isle of Mull/St. Andrew Pipes & Drums
Colorado Lawyers for the Arts
Colorado Mahlerfest
Colorado Music Festival
Colorado New Music Association
Colorado Photographic Arts Center
Colorado Railroad Museum
Colorado Symphony Association

Colorado Symphony Guild
Colorado Wildlife Federation
Colorado Wind Ensemble
Colorado Youth Pipe Band
Colorado Youth Symphony Orchestra
Columbine Chorale
Commerce City Cultural Council
Creative Coalition
Creative Music Works
Crossover Project-MultiCultural Network
CSA Ballet Foundation
Curtis School Arts & Humanities Center
Dance Advantage
David Taylor Dance Theatre
Denver Art Museum
Denver Audubon Society
Denver Black Arts Festival
Denver Botanic Gardens
Denver Brass
Denver Center Media
Denver Center Theatre Company
Denver Chamber Choir
Denver Civic Theatre
Denver Concert Band
Denver Firefighters Museum
Denver Gay Mens Chorus
Denver International Film Society
Denver March Powwow
Denver Municipal Band
Denver Museum of Miniatures, Dolls & Toys
Denver Museum of Natural History
Denver Rail Heritage Society
Denver Urban Forest
Denver Young Artists Orchestra
Denver Zoo City Park
Douglas County Council for the Arts & Humanities
Downtown Aurora Visual Arts
EDEN Theatrical Workshop
El Centro Su Teatro
Eldorado Springs Historical Society
Englewood Cultural Center
Englewood Recreation Services
Erie Historical Society
Eulipions, Inc.
Evergreen Area Council for the Arts Evergreen
Chamber Orchestra
Evergreen Children's
Evergreen Chorale, Inc.
Evergreen Players
First Night Colorado
Flatirons Art Center
Foothills Art Center
Foothills Park & Rec. District
Forney Transportation Museum
Four Mile Historic Park
Free Flyght Center for the Arts
Frequent Flyers Productions, Inc.
Friends of Chamber Music
Friends of Dinosaur Ridge
Friends of the School of the Arts
Germinal Stage
Golden Area Historical Association
Golden DAR Pioneer Museum
Gould Voice Research Center
Hannah Kahn Dance Company
Heritage Fine Arts Guild of Arapahoe County
Highlands Ranch Community Chorus
Highlands Ranch Historical Society
Historic Boulder
Historic Denver, Inc.
Historic Frankstown
Historic Paramount Foundation
Hiwan Homestead Museum
Hunger Artists
Imagination Makers Theatre Co.
Industrial Arts Theatre
Jan Justis Dance Co.
Jefferson County Historical Society
Jefferson Symphony Orchestra
Jeppesen Aviation Foundation
Joey Favre Humanities Center
Ken Caryl Ranch Metropolitan District

Kim Robards Dance
Lafayette Cultural Arts Commission
Lafayette Historical Society, Inc.
Lakewood Arts Council
Lakewoods Historical Belmar Village
Littleton Children's Chorale
Littleton Choral Society
Littleton Historical Museum
Littleton Symphony
Littleton Town Hall Arts Center
Longmont Chorale, Inc.
Longmont Council for the Arts
Longmont Museum
Longmont Symphony Orchestra
Longmont Theatre Company
Louisville Art Association
Louisville Arts & Humanities Council
Lyons Arts & Humanities Council
Magic Moments, Inc.
Main Street Players
Mayor's Office of Art, Culture and Film
Melvin Schoolhouse Museum-Library
Mizel Museum of Judaica
Molly Brown House Museum
Morrison Theater Company
Mostly Strauss Orchestra
Moyo Nguvu Cultural Arts Center
Museo de Las Americas
Nederland Arts & Humanities Advisory Board
Nomad Players, Inc.
Northglenn Arts & Humanities Foundation
Northland Chorale
Opera Colorado
Paletteers Art Club, Inc.
Parker Area Historical Society
Parker Cultural Commission
Peanut Butter Players
Performance Inventions
Physically Handicapped Amateur Musical Actors
    League (PHAMALY)
Pirate: A Contemporary Art Oasis
Pleasant Plains Country School
Robert Garner Center Attractions
Rocky Mountain Brassworks
Rocky Mountain Chapter, American Theatre
    Organ Society
Rocky Mountain Chorale
Rocky Mountain Jewish Historical Society
Rocky Mountain Quilt Museum
Rocky Mountain Ragtime Festival
Rocky Mountain Repertory Ensemble
Rocky Mountain Symphony
Rocky Mountain Women's Institute
Schoolhouse Museum/Cherry Creek
Shadow Mountain Center for the Arts
South Suburban Cultural Arts Division
South Suburban Theatre Company
South Suburban—South Platte Park
Southwest Creative Dance Center
Spare Time Players, Inc.
Spark Cooperative Gallery
St. Cecilia Singers
St. Vrain Historical Society
Stage Eleven Suite
Summit Jazz Foundation
Swallow Hill Music Association
Teatro Latino De Colorado
The Museum of Outdoor Arts
Theater in the Park
Theatre On Broadway
Thornton Arts, Sciences & Humanities Council
UHURU SASA Institute of African Studies
Upstart Crow Theatre Company
Very Special Arts Colorado
Village Arts Coalition
Vistas of Time
Westminster Area Historical Society
Westminster Community Artist Series
Wheat Ridge Historical Museum
Wheat Ridge Historical Society
Young Audiences, Inc.
Younger Generation Players

171

INDEX